BARNSLEY STREETS 2

Loving wishes to my dear friend
for her love over many years.
Cicely.
14th. april 2003.

BARNSLEY STREETS

Volume 2

E. G. Tasker

Wharncliffe Publishing

First Published in 2002 by
Wharncliffe Books
an imprint of
Pen and Sword Books Limited,
47 Church Street, Barnsley,
South Yorkshire. S70 2AS

Copyright © Ted Tasker Photographic Trust 2002

For up-to-date information on other titles produced under the
Wharncliffe imprint, please telephone or write to:

Wharncliffe Books
FREEPOST
47 Church Street
Barnsley
South Yorkshire S70 2BR
Telephone (24 hours): 01226 - 734555

ISBN: 1-871647-96-7

A CIP catalogue record of this book is available from the
British Library

Printed in Great Britain by CPI UK

Contents

The last days of the Royal Oak in Peel Square.

INTRODUCTION

The updating and re-publication of Edward Tasker's 1970s series of booklets continues with this volume. Again we have included almost all the illustrations from the originals whilst adding up-to-date photographs taken by Raymond Walker.

The maps included are from the Ordnance Survey 1:2500 edition of the early 1960s, plus extracts from the latest edition for comparison. The O.S. maps since 1960 have the advantage of showing the street numbers of the properties. The latest editions are also used to show some dramatic changes to Barnsley's townscape since the 1960s; in this volume notably the rebuilding of Peel Street including the creation of Peel Parade, the building of the Westway relief road, and the arrival of the Alhambra shopping mall.

Philip Rawlings has continued his updating of the lists of occupants of all these town centre properties. These lists are Edward Tasker's unique contribution to Barnsley history, turning what would otherwise be another book of photographs into a powerful tool for anyone researching the history of our town.

How to use this book

The streets covered by this volume are shown on the contents page. In most cases one side of the street is covered in sequence, followed by the other side. Sections from Ordnance Survey maps are also provided to assist in identifying the streets and buildings.

The names of the occupants of buildings are listed as in the original books but these lists have been updated, in this volume to 2000/2001. It has not been possible to fill all the gaps between Mr Tasker's research and the present day but this information should still be found very useful in identifying business premises which have the occupier's name on the outside. It is also helpful in dating photographs, in this book or from other sources.

We have retained Mr Tasker's method of listing; the number of a building is shown at the top of the column. The occupiers are then listed below in date order, starting with the most recent. Where the street number of a property has changed the older number is inserted in the column, the occupiers using that number being listed below it. We have also retained Mr Tasker's style in showing dates of occupation with the more recent date first. For example number 6 Wellington Street was occupied by S. Brocklebank from 1895 to 1896, this is shown as '1896-1895 S. Brocklebank'.

ACKNOWLEDGMENTS

The Trustees of the Ted Tasker Photographic Collection Trust would like to express their thanks to the following:

The Archives and Legal Departments of Barnsley Metropolitan Borough Council for their continued support of the Trust.

Wharncliffe Publishing for their advice and assistance, and in particular their **Paul Wilkinson** for his patient work on our behalf.

Philip Rawlings for his research on behalf of the Trust into the occupancy of premises.

Our own Trustees; **Raymond Walker** for keeping the photographic record up to date and, with **Stuart Currie** for the work of collating the information and proof-reading and correcting the manuscript.

Mr Melvyn Hepworth for assistance in updating the lists of landlords of licensed premises.

The management of the Alhambra shopping mall for providing information on the occupiers of units, and in particular **Mrs Jan Czlapka** for her work in gathering and listing that information.

Mr John Porteous for his valuable help in telling the story of Hayes Croft.

And again, **Mrs Mary Tasker,** whose vision and enthusiasm made the formation of the Tasker Trust and therefore the publication of these volumes possible.

Errors

We are aware that despite our best efforts errors are bound to occur, or information be incomplete. We already know this to be true of Volume One. We would greatly value any assistance from readers in correcting these volumes. Information can be forwarded to:

The Ted Tasker Photographic Trust,
c/o Mrs Needham, Borough Secretary's Department,
Town Hall,
BARNSLEY. S70 2TA

Snow clearing in Peel Street about one hundred years ago.

PEEL SQUARE (FORMERLY PEASEHILL NOOK)

SOUTH SIDE

MARKET STREET

2

2001-1999 Leeds and Holbeck Building Society
1999-1988 A.A. Travel and Motor Insurance
1988-1984 Medina Footwear
1983-1973 Millets Clothing and Camping
1973-1965 Shapero Carpets
1964-1933 British Colonial Footwear Co.
1929-1857 M. Lowrance and Son Ironmongers

Crown Inn

1856-1851 Wm. Wagstaff
1850-1849 John Woodruff
1848-1847 Geo. Champion
1846-1841 Frederick Crow

Waggon and Horses

1839-1790 James Leadman

Peel Square
c 1960.

4

2001-1999 Arden News
1999-1995 Peel News
1995-1989 York Smokers Shop
1989-1980 Walco Footwear
1980-1969 Easiphit Shoes
1969-1965 John Temple Tailors
1964-1926 Service Tailoring Co.
1925-1920 Chas. A. Powell Tailor
1919-1884 Edward Cooke Corn Miller
1883-1880 Geo. Shaw
1871 Thomas Goodair Butcher
1868-1844 Geo Stringer Butcher

Queens Head Yard

1973-1925 Knights of the Golden Horn Club
1916-1898 John Pollit Bakehouse
1897-1894 Henry Higgins
1893-1892 J. Hinchcliffe Warehouse
1891 H. Haselhurst Warehouse
1887 J. Horbury
1882-1871 Thomas Steele Whitesmith
1871 Wm Stringer Town Crier

This photograph and the one opposite is a record of these shops in the 1960's. Builders Exchange appears to be a curious name for one of them. 'KGH' in the upper windows refers to the Knights of the Golden Horn Society.

6/8

2001-1993 Vision Value Opticians
1992-1989 Mad Harry Household Goods
1989-1986 Digby's Tobacco and General
1985-1968 Super Simon Stores
1964-1961 Lipton Ltd.

960-1929 F. Cornan
Tobacconist
925-1895 W. Bygate
Hairdresser
894 Matthew Francis
893 Aaron Axon

8

1960-1925 Lipton Ltd.
1925-1913 F. Cornan
Tobacconist
1913-1906 E. & E. Moody
Needlework
1905-1894 Cyclists Supply Co.
1893 J. Ibbotson

1892 Central Dinning Rooms
1896-1889 W. Hayselhurst
1887 Wm. Charlesworth
1886-1885 P. Casey

Queen Head Hotel

1883-1877 Ann Yates
1877-1869 Geo. Yates
1868-1861 Geo. Stringer
1860 Mark Ellis
1859-1835 Geo. Stringer
1833 Wm. Shields
1830 Wm. Brooke
1825 G. Shepherd

Old Royal Oak Yard

1956-1933 Tower Table
Mineral Water Co.
1932 Hattersley and Usher
1929-1925 Reynolds Bros.
Garage
1913-1900 Reynolds and Wadsworth
Warehouse
1888 W. S. Armitage
Warehouse

The brash cut price posters were a sign of the times in the 1960s. Above, a view in 2000.

In the 1960s the opening at the side of the Service tailoring Co. was still known as Queens Head Yard; illustrating how history lingers on in the retaining of a name.

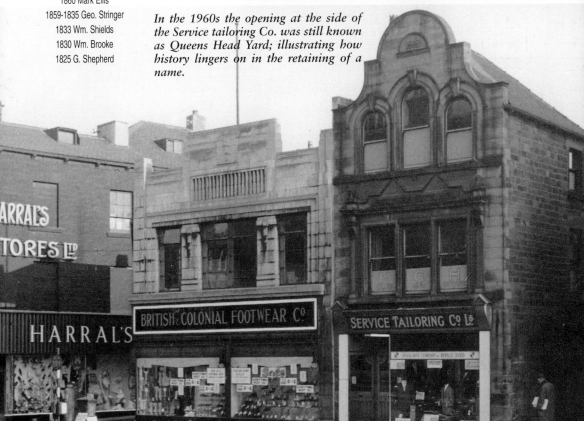

10

2001-1970 Casa Disco Records
1969-1962 Entrance

Imperial Hotel

Demolished 1960
1959-1957 Walter Collins
1957-1953 Alfred E. Halstead
1953-1948 Wm M. Savage
1948-1946 Fred Owram
1946-1945 Marion Owram
1945-1939 Fred Owram
1939-1936 Alan Wadsworth
1936-1929 Thomas R. Cranidge
1929-1928 Thomas Turner
1928-1927 John D. Jones
1927-1924 Will Coward
1924-1921 Harold A. S. Maygar
1921-1905 Geo. Parkes
1905-1903 Arthur Taylor

10

1901-1882 John Midgley Butcher
1881 Thomas H. Hobson
1880-1860 Thomas Abson

12

2001-1996 William Hills Betting Shop
1996-1980 Provincial Building Society
1980 Vacant
1979-1973 B.B.C.S. Bank
1972-1969 B.B.C.S. Chemists
1968-1962 Meadow Self Service

12

1960-1929 R. M. Hill Jeweller
1929-1914 H. M. Cleverley
1913 Clement Chappell
1912-1911 T. McNeil Butcher
1910 R. W. Dank Butcher

14

2001-1996 Johnsons Cleaners
1995-1986 Crockatts Cleaners
1985-1962 Zerny Dry Cleaning

16

2001-2000 Stanley Racing
2000-1986 Parthenon 2 Restaurant
1985-1962 Aloha Coffee Bar

――――――――――――――――― Demolished 1960 ―――――――――――――――――

Above

1959-1929 Geo. Berry & Son Opticians
1929 J. C. Ward
1925 W. H. Walker Ladies Hairdresser
1924-1922 E. Lawson Wireless Engineer
1914 G. A. Charlton Dentist
1908 G. W. Howcroft Accountant

14

1960-1934 L. Frances Hairdresser
1933-1924 John Hale Hatter
1923-1911 J. H. Booth Hatter
1910-1906 Ann Tomlinson Confectioner

――――――――――――――――――― Old Royal Oak ―――――――――――――――――――

1901 James Axon	1889-1888 Henry Burgess	1883-1882 John Savage	1855-1854 Elizabeth Pickering
1901-1899 Arthur Allenby	1888-1887 John Wm. Bridge	1882-1877 Charles Townend	1852-1842 Isaac Dennis
1899-1898 Mary Crossley	1887-1886 David C. Bridge	1877-1875 Edmund Fields	1841-1822 John Winter
1898-1890 John Crossley	1886-1885 Henry Shepherd	1874-1860 Geo. Wilkinson	
1890-1889 Walter Lockwood	1885-1883 Thomas Aspin	1859-1856 Edward Abson	

The death throes of the Old Royal Oak and the adjoining butchers shop, the window of which is hidden by the striped blind.

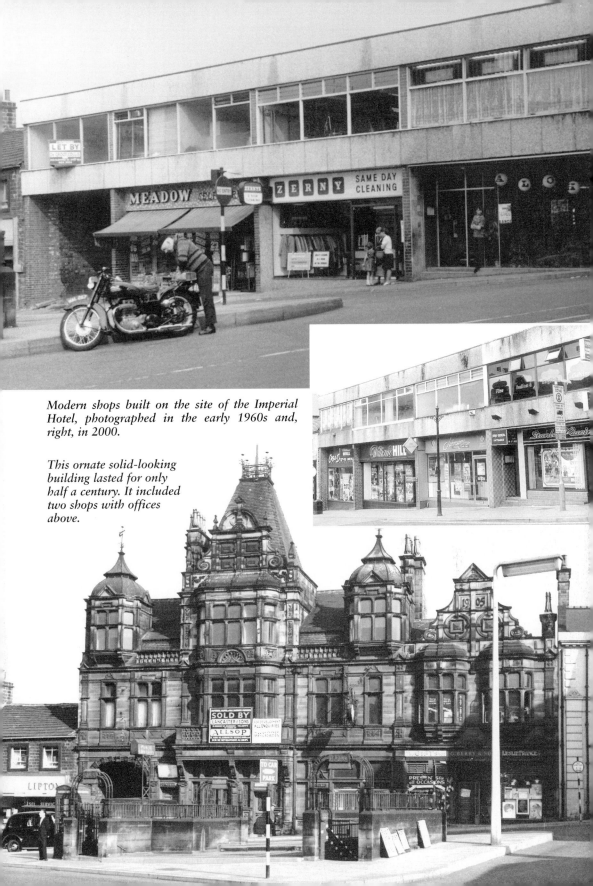

Modern shops built on the site of the Imperial Hotel, photographed in the early 1960s and, right, in 2000.

This ornate solid-looking building lasted for only half a century. It included two shops with offices above.

Corner Pin Hotel

2001 Les Hall

1972-1971 John Charlesworth	1929-1928 John A. Wordsworth
1971-1970 Thomas Johnson	1928-1923 Henry Turner
1970-1968 Philip Marsland	1923-1917 Samuel S. T. Smith
1968 Patrick Cummins	1917-1903 Alice E. Skelton
1968-1965 Wm. B. Scotting	1903-1898 Amos Skelton
1965-1963 Donald M. Harrison	1898-1892 Tom Crow
1963-1962 Stanley Lockyer	1892-1886 Tom Savage
1962-1960 Wm. Merryweather	1886-1884 Thomas Elliott
1960-1956 Peter Stott Jnr.	1884-1877 Joseph Mitchell
1956-1954 Peter Stott	1877 Samuel Gill
1954-1942 Frank Greenwood	1877 John Freeman
1942-1931 Lawrence H. Baker	1877-1875 Jane Steele
1931-1929 Herbert Ellison	1875-1870 Henry Steel

Three Horse Shoes

1870-1864 Christopher Harding
1863 Edwin Rock
1862 Joseph Smith
1861-1852 Richard Freeman
1851-1848 Richard Tomlin
1847 Geo. Wood
1846-1842 Isaac Fox
1841 Thomas Senior Butcher
1839-1833 Robert Gelder Butcher
1830 Geo. Craven
1825 James Patrick

The present Corner Pin seen here in 1960, replaced the earlier building seen opposite in 1912. Although it faces Peel Square the address is 2 Wellington Street.

The poster is advertising a play 'The Bad Girl of the Family' then being presented at the
Theatre Royal in Wellington Street. Below, the same view in 2001.

Two milk floats wait in the Square with horse-drawn cabs, but the car approaching from Pitt Street is a sign of things to come. E. & E. Moody occupied number 8 between 1906 and 1913.

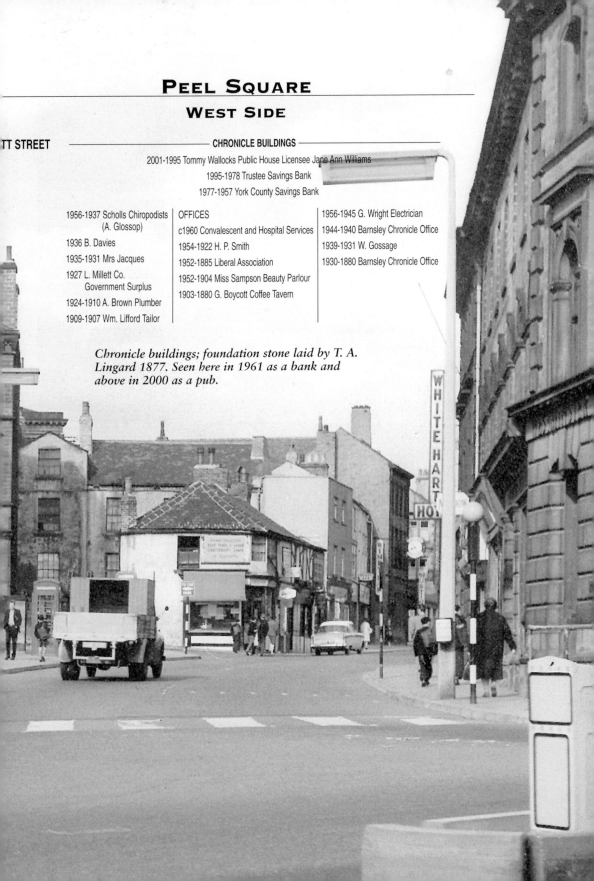

PEEL SQUARE

WEST SIDE

TT STREET

CHRONICLE BUILDINGS

2001-1995 Tommy Wallocks Public House Licensee Jane Ann Williams

1995-1978 Trustee Savings Bank

1977-1957 York County Savings Bank

1956-1937 Scholls Chiropodists
(A. Glossop)

1936 B. Davies

1935-1931 Mrs Jacques

1927 L. Millett Co.
Government Surplus

1924-1910 A. Brown Plumber

1909-1907 Wm. Lifford Tailor

OFFICES

c1960 Convalescent and Hospital Services

1954-1922 H. P. Smith

1952-1885 Liberal Association

1952-1904 Miss Sampson Beauty Parlour

1903-1880 G. Boycott Coffee Tavern

1956-1945 G. Wright Electrician

1944-1940 Barnsley Chronicle Office

1939-1931 W. Gossage

1930-1880 Barnsley Chronicle Office

Chronicle buildings; foundation stone laid by T. A. Lingard 1877. Seen here in 1961 as a bank and above in 2000 as a pub.

A few of the postcards sold by Mr. Raynor at number one have survived and some have been used in this history of the Streets of Barnsley.

PEEL SQUARE
NORTH SIDE

3

2001-1999 Greggs PLC Sandwich Shop
1999-1970 Radio Rentals
1970-1957 Rentaset
1956 Symington Ltd.
1954-1931 A. E. Sisson Butcher
1931-1923 Salter and Salter Footwear
1923-1917 H. M. Morris Fancy Draper
1916 Feasby and Garner
1915-1912 H. N. Booker Taxis
1912-1897 London City and Midland Bank
1896 Miles S. Walsh
1895 J. W. Ogden
1894-1890 Joseph Holden Co Tailors
1889-1857 Harriet Medlam Hosier

1

2001-1990 'Birthdays' Cards
1989-1986 Card Cavern Cards
1985-1962 Goodworth's Confectioners
1960-1947 Meadow Diary Co.
1935-1910 Walter Neale and Son Printers
1909-1902 J. Raynor Co. Printers
1900-1897 Walter Neale Printers
1896-1884 G. Shaw Printer
1883-1874 Geo. M. Bane Outfitter
1873-1872 Rolf Harrison Tailor

13

1871-1862 Reynor Bros. Drapers
1861-1857 John Bygate Boot Maker

Peel Square in about 1914 and, above, in 2000.

In 1840 on this site were several smaller buildings including a bakehouse kept by Henry Machon. Shortly afterwards these were pulled down.

This part of the hotel was built before the other part. it replaced an earlier inn.

7

Demolished c1924

1923-1922 M. Cleverley Confectioner

1921-1918 Midland Army Stores

1916-1896 S. E. Clarkson Confectioner

1895-1892 S. E. Medlam Confectioner

1891-1889 Medlam and Popplewell Confectioners

1888-1880 Medlam and Shoesmith Confectioners

5

2001-1989 Macey's Public House Licencee Malcolm Thompson

1989- White Hart Hotel

1973-1963 Geo. Marsh	1901-1884 Emma Smith
1963-1959 Walter Collins	1883-1851 Henry Smith
1959-1949 Geo. L. Brown	1850 Wm. Wilkinson
1949-1940 Angus C. Seed	1849-1847 James Brown
1940-1932 Ernest Beecroft	1846-1833 Wm. Ward
1932 Ethel M. Elstone	1830 Geo. Ridsdale
1933-1925 Thomas Elstone	1825 Joseph Ridsdale
1925-1922 Charles Foster	1822 E. Ridsdale
1922-1910 Thomas Armitage	SIX RINGERS INN
1910-1908 Gertrude Slim	Thomas Jackson
1908-1901 Alexander W. Slim	Thomas Kenyon
1901 Ernest Smith	

The style of lettering and the dress of the ladies and the children add to the atmosphere of this shop as it was a hundred years ago.

The scene in front of the White Hart Hotel in the years before the Great War, when the horse-drawn cab was still in competition with the newly introduced motor taxi. Mr Burkinshaw not only advertised his profession but also his hours of working.

Graham's Orchard	13/11	9	7
	2001-1978 Co-op Bank	2001-1989 Storey's Amusements	2001-1991 Storey's Amusements
	1978 Under Construction Co-op Bank	1988 Vacant	1991-1986 Barnsley Chronicle News Offi
B.B.C.S. Booking Office	B.B.C.S. Taxis	1987-1977 Courtney's Fabrics	1985-1952 Albert Hirst Butcher
1949-1933 A. Walters Tobacconist	1942-1933 G. Booker Ltd. Taxis	1976-1973 Telesure	1951-1935 Modern Butchers
1933-1920 E. and A. Hatton Sweets-Tobacco	1932 C. H. Webb	1973-1932 Taylor's Radio	1935-1931 P. Smith Butcher
	1930 Shafton Motor Co.	1932-1924 L. Millett Government Surplus	1929-1927 Varley Bros.
	1927-1920 Hatton Bros. Central Garage		1927-1925 Quick Press
	1917-1913 Barnsley Motor Co.		1925 J. W. Hallatt
	1912-1897 C. A. Fox Cab Proprietor		1925 S. Mills
	1869-1860 Coach and Horses Mews		

1923-1882 Reynolds and Wadsworth

		1877-1862 Thomas Lingard Printer	1877-1856 Thomas Lingard Printer
		1861-1859 Charles Johnson	
		1857-1855 G. Ward	

The presence of cart horses in Peel Square is a reminder that Barnsley was an agricultural centre and the importance of this breed of horses for pulling heavy loads. On the left can be seen the rather odd frontage of Reynolds and Wadsworths, demolished c.1924. Property numbers were also altered at that time

The White Hart was extended and the two shops were built c.1924 after the warehouse previously occupied by Messrs. Reynolds and Wadsworth was pulled down.

The news vendor always favoured this spot from which to sell his papers. In 1978 these buildings were replaced by the Co-op Bank, seen on the opposite page.

GRAHAMS ORCHARD

WEST SIDE

19

2001-1996 Premier Taxis

1996-? Insurance Office

?-? BSM School of Motoring

11

2001-1999 '2001' Pro Body Piercing Studio

1999-? Hotch Potch Art & Gift Shop

?-? Sports Shop

?-1973 Brinsleys Estate Agents

17 (above 11)

2001-1983 Barnsley Insurance & Mortgages Agents

1983-? Penistone Insurance

?-1973 Geoffrey Robinson Photographer

9/7

2001-2000 'Top That' Pizzas

2000-1982 Stanley Racing Betting Shop

15 (above 9)

2001-1973 A. Whiteley Optician

ALL REBUILT EARLY 1970s

This is a view of Grahams Orchard looking towards Peel Square in c1960 when some demolition had alredy taken place

13 (above 7) | **Peel Parade** | **Car Park**

2001-1993 Cut Above Hair Studio

1993-? Hair Salons

?-1973 Makinsons Driving School

By the end of the 1960's new buildings can be seen, and the area cleared for a car park and the entrance to Peel Parade.

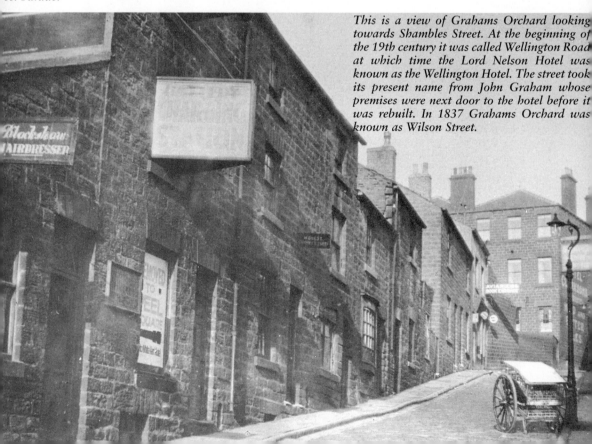

This is a view of Grahams Orchard looking towards Shambles Street. At the beginning of the 19th century it was called Wellington Road at which time the Lord Nelson Hotel was known as the Wellington Hotel. The street took its present name from John Graham whose premises were next door to the hotel before it was rebuilt. In 1837 Grahams Orchard was known as Wilson Street.

GRAHAMS ORCHARD

EAST SIDE

Only two premises operating on this side

Not numbered

Rear of Orchard Brewery Bar (on Market Hill)

8

2001-? Brownes Bar

? name change from Temple of The Muses

Temple of the Muses

1973-1960 Donald Harrison	1901-1900 John Oxley	1892-1890 James Lee	1867-1864 John Wilkinson	1848 Martha Shearwood
1960-1959 Patrick Kenny	1900-1899 Arthur D. Pitt	1890-1884 Joshua Hampson	1863-1862 Joseph R. Horsfield	1847-1845 William Shearwood
1959-1920 Thomas Kenny	1899-1898 Barker Artle	1884-1877 Geo. Jackson	1861 D. Mahony	
1920-1915 John Lavelle	1898-1897 Ben Senior	1877-1876 James Jones	1860-1857 Joseph Gawthorpe	1844 James Brierley
1915-1914 Emma Ryan	1897-1895 Thomas Worth	1876 Charles Rose	1856 Edward Abson	1842-1841 Morley
1914-1905 Pat Ryan	1895-1893 Benjamin Naylor	1876 Charles Townend	1855-1854 John Woodruff	1838-1837 Mrs. Greaves
1905-1901 Bartholomew Kelly	1893-1892 Geo. Hepplestall	1876-1868 George Brown	1852-1849 James Denton	1835-1825 Charles Greaves

The main entrance to the Temple of the Muses now called Brownes Bar, is in Grahams Orchard. It can be reached also from Market Hill by a narrow passage. Patrick Kenny was the licensee when this photograph was taken in 1960. His father who preceded him was landlord for forty years.

The corner shop was built in 1888; it has been a chemist's shop since 1929.

This super market replaced the three small shops illustrated in the photograph above, and numbers 9 and 11 alongside. In the year 2000, opposite, the view is much the same.

PEEL STREET

NORTH SIDE

11 / 9 / 7 / 5 / 3

2001-1995 Walmsley"s Suite Superstore

1994-1993 Vacant

1993-1988 Wilkinson Home and Garden Supplies

1987-1976 Presto Supermarket

1976-1964 Lipton's Supermarket

Rebuilt 1964

1

1st Floor	2nd Floor
2001-1993 Peel Street Barbers	2001-1986 E. N. Smith Jewellery Manufacturer and repair
1993-? Paul Wilkinson Barber	
?-? Ron Dale Barber	

1	**9**	**7**	**5**	**3**	
960-1945 R. Midgley Pet Shop	1960 I. Walker Antiques	1960-1906 H. Dale Hairdresser	1960 Lodge and Hughes Overalls	1960-1928 J. W. Bailey Saddler	2001-1997 Superdrug
944-1880 Stephenson Painter	1959-1956 J. R. Steele Building Supplies		1959-1955 Misses Langdale	1927-1925 Salter & Salter Footwear	1996 Clinichem
393 W. E.	1955-1948 I. Walker Antiques	1905 Fred Hinchliffe Hairdresser	1954-1950 Harold L. Wharam	1922-1908 W. Randall Photographer	1996-1946 G. H. Rock Ltd Chemists
	1947-1945 J. Winstanley	1902 I. Pearl Wardrobe Dealer	1949-1948 M. Butler Dressmaking	1905 Fred C. Neale Printer	1946-1932 Alfred Green Chemist
	1944 Bielby and Evans	1900 John Jennings	1945 Forest Electrical Co.	1894-1893 J. E. Gelder	1931-1929 E. Nash Chemist
	1940-1937 R. N. Fitton Ltd.	1897 James Hudson	1944 J. R. Steele	1892-1890 Joseph Gaunt	1928-1922 G. W. Rogerson Outfitter
	1937-1935 N. Lee Draper	1895-1874 Charles Ogley	1940-1937 Beverleys Ltd. Wine & Spirits	1887 T. & L. Stephenson	1922 G. A. Nicholson Tailor
	1935-1934 F. Whitehouse Ladies Outfitter	New Property	1936 Waring and Cutts		1920-1899 E. Weissenrieder Brush Maker
	1934-1912 E. Rowey Milliner		1935-1931 A. Walters Confectioner		1898 Thomas Proctor Draper
	1911-1882 Wm. C. Fevers Tailor		1930 Louise Smith		1896 Newtons Fent Warehouse
	1880-1875 Barnsley Newspaper Co.		1929-1913 A. Wright Confectioner		1893-1891 Mark Booker
			1912-1904 E. Charlesworth Fruiterer		1888 Wm. Edwards
			1902-1898 H. E. Cawthorne Green Grocer		
			1895 James Bradbury		
			1892-1873 Joseph Green		

1871 F. W. Cooke Basket Maker
1869-1860 Charles Halton
1859-1840 Joseph Firth Clothes Broker

1871-1860 Charles Ogley Fishmonger
1859-1842 John Ostcliffe
1841-1839 Mrs Atkinson

These Victorian shops with living accommodation above are typical of the period. The large buildings to the left, then Jackson's Stores, still stands in 2001 as can be seen opposite.

It is interesting to compare the new and old form of transport. The fashionable lady appears to be intrigued by the new arrival. This is between 1906 and 1911.

17/13

2001-1988 Iceland Frozen Foods
1988-1986 Times Furniture and Carpets
1985-1962 Cavendish Furniture Store
1961-1939 Jackson's Furniture Store

Dog Lane

17

1935-1891 George Rhymer
1890-1881 Saul C. Chappell
1880 Christopher Alexander
1874-1860 Thomas Summers Rope Walk

15

1937-1925 Frank Cornan Tobacconist
1925-1923 Midland Army Stores
1922-1906 R. A. Barritt Draper
1905-1887 James Wood Chemist
1886 Wm. Charlesworth
1885-1834 Thomas G. Harper
1883-1881 Smith and Armitage
1880-1879 Mary N. Senior

13

1938-1908 Jacksons Furniture Store
1907-1881 J. and P. Hindson Corn Merchant
1880-1879 Edwin Gelder

Peel Street in 1960 and 2001

Reproduced from the Ordnance Survey map with the permission of Ordnance Survey on behalf of Her Majesty's Stationery Office, © Crown Copyright MC 100035068

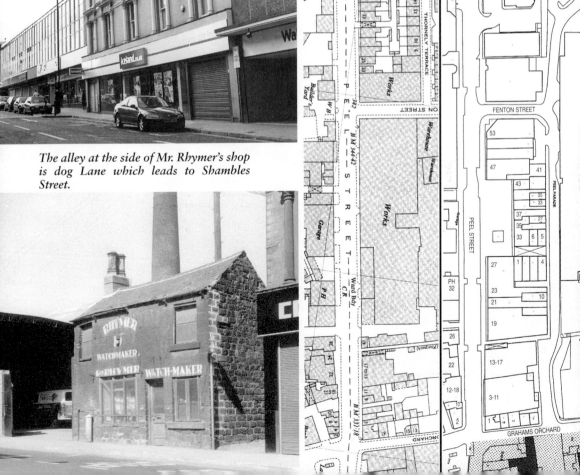

The alley at the side of Mr. Rhymer's shop is dog Lane which leads to Shambles Street.

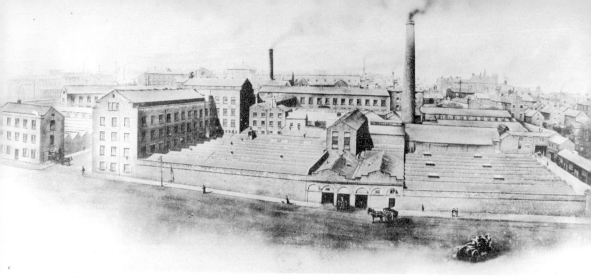

Taylor's Factory.

Its interesting to compare these two pictures. All these factory premises were demolished in the 1970's and replaced by the present parade of shops numbered 19 to 43, seen opposite.

21	**19**	**Dog Lane**
2001-1978 Jonathan James Footwear	2001-1985 Argos Distributors	
1978-1976 St. Clair Household Goods	1985-1982 M.F.I. Furniture	
	1982-1976 Status Wallpaper and Paints	

1975-1970 Home Building Cash and Carry

—————— Ex Taylors Factory rebuilt 1970s ——————

1960-1931 Yorkshire Tyre Rubber Co.

1905 Sheffield Butchers   1905 T. Attewell
Hide & Skin Co.   Blacksmith

19

1960-1948 G. Rhymer Watchmaker

1922 J. Rank Ltd. Office

1912 G. Booker Taxi Office

1905-1878 Wm. Potter

1871 Wm Stringer Carriers Agent

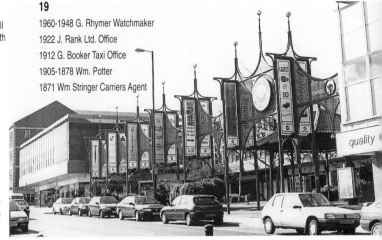

The traditonal miner's demonstration complete with banners and bands makes its way along Peel St.

27/23

2001-2000 Quality Save Discount Household Store

2000-1996 Harvey's Furniture

1996-1982 Cantors Furniture/Carpets

27/25

1982-1976 Cantors Furniture/Carpets

23

1982-1976 White Rose T.V./Electrical

1976 Roy's T.V./Electrical

————————— Ex Taylors Factory Rebuilt 1970's —————————

The tall building at the corner of Fenton Street was for some years all that remained of what was Taylor's Mill.

The house on the right, previously described as 'one of the narrowest in the town', is now thought to have been an extension to the main house.

43-41	39	37	35	33	Entry
					Peel
					Parade
2001-1995 Cash Converters	2001-1996 Scrivens Optical Hearing Centre	2001-1992 Oriental City Chinese Restaurant	2001-2000 The Money Shop	2001-1982 K3 Cosmetic Dental Studio	
Amusement Arcade	B.P. Ryder Opticians	Golden Crown Chinese Restaurant	Alliance Assurance Company	Kitchens Music Shop	

Ex Taylors Facttory rebuilt 1970's

Part of the parade of shops numbered 33-43.

Numbers 45. This picture should be compared with the one below. Built in 1877 by the Barnsley British Co-operative Society, this was one of their earliest branches.

Town End Roundabout

Unit 1

2001-1997 K.F.C. Kentucky Fried Chicken

Both Worlds Petrol Station

──────────── Rebuilt 1970s and 1980s ────────────

| 47 | 45 | | 25 |

47

1962-1956 S. D. Tyas Sweets
1955-1946 Clifford Wigley Books
1946 J.P. Shaw
1944 E. Winstanley
1943 E. Bielby
1942 Ivy Cotton
1941-1939 G. A. Gascoyne
1939-1934 P. Wilson Circulating Library
1933 H. Barton
1929-1927 L. Goldthorpe Fried Fish
1926-1923 E. Pyne
1922-1917 A. E. Bray Fried Fish
1915-1913 M. Shortland

1912-1911 J. Swift Fried Fish
1910 S. Taylor
1909-1908 Wm. Lord
1907 Thomas Stenton
1906-1900 J. Knight Fried Fish
1896-1894 Joseph Hunt
1893 - Nicholson
1889-1888 J. Popplewell
1887-1881 Wm. M. Malcolm
1880 Wm. Bennett
1879-1863 Geo. Thornley
1862 Charles Carr
1861-1856 Geo. Price Shopkeeper

45

1968- Kingsway Confectionery Cash & Carry

1963-1877 B.B.C.S. Grocers

1973-1968 K. Jackson Radio Television

1963-1942 B.B.C.S. Butchers

1942-1877 B.B.C.S. Grocers

Numbers 27 to 43 consisted of a row of houses built in 1902 and pulled down in 1970. Amongst them was one very small house.

25

1968-1956 Hy. Elsto Sweets-T

1955-1935 P. A. Ethe Confectic

1933 R. W. Elvin
1932 S. Stanyard
1929 C. Peck Fried
1926 A. Brook
1923 J. H. Pembertc
1922-1905 W. R. Wh Fried Fish

1868-1860 Wm. Robinson

Stone Yard

PEEL STREET

WRIGHT'S TOWN END DISPENSARY

WRIGH CHEMISTS Chemist WRIGHT

DISPENSING

WRIGHT. PHARMACEUTICAL CHEMIST

Unit 2	59	Fenton St.	53	51-47
2001-1998 Blockbuster Entertainment	2001-1992 Job Centre (Cooper House)		2001 Riley's Quality furniture	2001-1998 Pound Stretcher
			2000-1998 Queensland Furniture	Waremart
			Porky's Nightclub and Bar	Dunnes
			The Stables Nightclub and Bar	Simco

——————— Rebuilt 1970s and 1980s ———————

——————— Ex Taylors Factory rebuilt 1970's ———————

1962-1946 W. Freeman & Co. Ltd

1945 Ridgeway & Co.

3	21
1973-1935 G. Wright Electrician	1973-1970 Home Building Cash & Carry
1929-1912 Carr and Waterhouse Cycle Agents	1969-1962 Builders Wares Ltd.
1911 J. W. Woodcock	Lower storey converted into shop
1909 Elijah Smith Cycle Dealer	1960 W. Freeman Co. Ltd.
1906-1891 John Snowball General Dealer	1945-1943 W. Ridgway and Son
1887 Charles Hopper	1943-1902 Brown and Rose Clothiers
1886-1884 Charles Howden	
1883 Albert Haigh	

1870-1860 Joseph Smith
Saw Pit

BOVRIL
at bedtime

for fitness
without fatness

S.D. TYAS

This area where six streets meet is known as Town End. The properties seen here were demolished to build the roundabout, seen in the photograph above.

From Peel Square that part of Peel Street formerly known as Mill Lane can be seen up to the Millstone Inn and the Corn Mill. Photographed between 1906 and 1913.

PEEL STREET

SOUTH SIDE

2	4	6	8	10	10 Upstairs
	2001-1978 T. W. Davison Jeweller (now 2-8)			2001 The Lunch Club Sandwich Shop	2001-1983 Level 2 Unisex Hair Salon
	1978 Vacant	1978-1955 T. W. Davison Jeweller		2000-1998 Dave Penty Sandwich Shop	
1977-1975 M. T. Greenwood Personal Loans Insurance				Vacant	
1974-1965 A. E. Gray Newsagent				1999-1991 Phuture Records	
-1934 J. Vetch Butcher	1960-1954 R. Freeman	1955-1900 T. W. Davison Jeweller	1955-1953 R. Freeman	1991-1988 MicroFun Computer Games (from Sheffield Rd)	
-1905 Eastman Ltd. Butchers	1953-1923 W. Sample Footwear	1899 W. M. Taylor Watchmaker	1952-1913 F. Simmons Newsagent	1987-1980 Mr. Giovanni Ladies Hairdresser	
-1893 Wm. G. Paxton Boot Maker	1922-1920 Sample and Boust Footwear	1878 J. White	1912-1900 H. Caffrey Newsagent	1979 Coverlight Blinds	
J. Senior	1915 Dan Hatton	1877-1875 John S. Harrison	1899-1880 T. Hepworth Newsagent	1978-1975 M.I.R. Supplies	
-1887 Samuel Fieldsend	1914 I. Pearl Ford Dealer	1874 Wm. Potter		1974-1957 Electro Medical Supplies	
John White	1913-1850 Samuel Newton Draper	1873 John Cotton	1880 Henry Gray	1956 E. E. Green	
-1874 Fred Harrison	1879 Fred Cawdill	1872 Joseph Green Fruiterer	1879 Samuel Newton	1955-1951 J. R. Farrar	
-1871 Wm. Freeman	1878 Edson and Allas		1878 B. Waddington	1950 Pat Kelly	
Joseph Wray	1877 Blackshaw and Loveland		1877-1875 Wm. Gaunt	1949-1941 W. J. Morris	
	1875-1873 John White		1874-1872 G. Blackburn	1940 Fred Smith	
	1872-1871 Edwin Gomersall		1871 Wm. Fernside	1939 B. W. Moore	
	1870-1868 James McLintock		1870 Henry Park	1929-1922 I. Pearl Clothier	
				1915-1914 Arthur Groom	
				1913-1908 R. C. Sampson Hairdresser	
				1906-1875 Geo. Fogg Hairdresser	
				1874-1863 Jabez Gomersall Hairdresser	

Before Peel Street was developed this area was considered to be part of Peel Square.

This photograph was taken in 1960 when numbers 12 and 14 were being reconstructed.

An organ grinder with his monkey opposite the Freemans Arms.

12/14/16/18

2001-1997 Quasimodos Bar/Restaurant

1997-1990 Franklins Restaurant

1989-1986 Vacant

1985-1982 Yoko Video House Amusements

1981-1973 Vacant

## 12/14	## 16/18
1973-1961 Cantors Ltd	Joined with 12/14 1978-1957 Cantors Ltd

───────── Rebuilt c1960 ─────────

1957-1919 I. Pearl & Son Clothiers   1957-1924 I. Pearl & Son Clothiers

12	**14**	**16**	**18**
1915-1904 W. G. Paxton Clogger	1920-1901 Isaac Pearl Clothier	1921-1901 Isaac Pearl Clothier	Wm. Ayston Fruiterer
1902-1896 Samuel Longbottom Clogger	1900 Edwin Huck		1909-1908 J. P. Hudson Corn Merchant
1895-1886 John Swift	1899- Bejamin Carr		1907 E. Reeson
1885-1884 Wm. Finkell	1892 Wm. Rust		1906 G. W. Cooper
1883 T. G. Harper	1888 Thomas Cooper		
1882-1877 Christopher Sharpe	1887-1886 T. G. Harper		**Freemans Arms**
1876-1871 John Hodgson Basket Maker	1885 John Swift		1903-1899 Joseph Hunt
1870-1869 Edwin Gomersall	1884 Thomas Mosley		1899-1896 Wm. Ogley
1868-1863 Joseph Payne	1883 Thomas Cooper		1896-1895 James Atkinson
1861 G. Broadhead	1882 T. G. Harper		1895-1886 George Smith
	1878 Tom Needham		1886-1885 Wm. Padgett
	1877-1875 Christopher Sharpe		1885 Joseph Smith
	1874 Joseph Wray Boot Maker		1884 Charles Ward
	1869-1865 Robt. Harrison Tailor		1883-1879 Samuel Gill
	1864-1863 Wm. Bexon		1878 Hannah Kilner
	1861-1855 Wm. Nichols		
		1877 John Charlesworth	**Freemans Arms**
		1872-1871 Henry Park	1877 James Kilner
		1870-1864 Wm. Freeman	1876-1872 John Stenton
		1861-1860 Ann Tetley	1871 Sarah Bexon
		1859-1857 J. Hattersley	1862-1861 Richard Mitchell
		1856 Charles Johnson	1860-1858 Geo. Broadhead
			1857-1855 Wm. Freeman

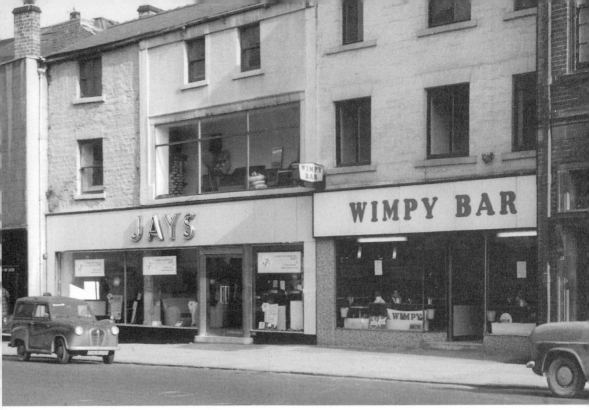

Numbers 20 to 26 in 1960.

In 1960 the remains of the old corn mill were still visible at number 30.

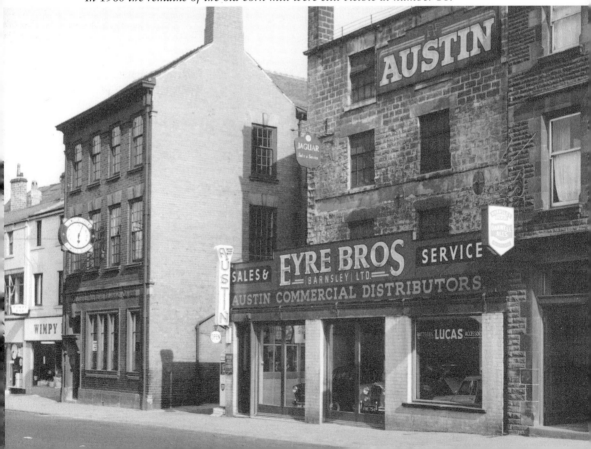

20/22

2001-1996 Dennis Peters House of Pine
1996-1990 South Yorkshire Furnishers
1990-1985 Furniture Trade Warehouse
1984-1976 South Yorkshire Furnishers
1975-1974 Discount Furnishers
1974-1968 Wainwrights Furniture
1967-1948 Jays Furniture

24/26

2001-2000 Budget Insurance
2000-1995 Century Insurance Centre
1995-1980 Penistone Insurance Co.
1980-1974 Caprice Ladies Wear
1973-1960 Wimpy Bar
1960-1948 J. R. Steele Ltd. Builders Suppliers

28

2001-1987 Herbert Brown
Jeweller and Pawn Brokers
1987-1978 Carrs Jewellers
1978-1974 Starlight Lampshades
1973-1962 Yorkshire   1973-1962 T. Horsfield
Mutual   Florist
Trading Co.
UPPER   LOWER
1962 Lower storey made into a shop
1962-1925 Yorkshire Mutual Trading Co.
pulled down
1925 Dan Hatton Sale Room
1916 W. Sowerby   1916 Dan Hatton

Millstone Inn

1912-1891 George Booker
1891 Mary Jane Nixon
1891-1879 Wm. Sparkes
1878 Alfred Carr
1877-1876 Jerimiah Edgar
1875-1869 John Daniel

20

1947-1945 J. R. Steele Ltd.
Builders Suppliers
1939-1936 H. Louth
Central Workshop
1936-1933 Cabinet Makers
Supply Store
1932-1930 E. Lawson
Wireless Dept.
1928-1923 Herbert Frank
Furniture Dealer
1922-1920 G. W. Scott Butcher
1918 J. Jepson
1917 W. H. Brown
1916-1882 W. Gainster
Provision Dealer
1881-1880 Charles Hy
Charlesworth
1878 Rebuilt
1877 Hiram Hutchinson
1875 Elizabeth Wilks

22

1947-1939 Jays Furniture
1938-1932 H. Lewis & Son
Furniture Mart
1929 F. E. Harrison
Refreshment Rooms
1926-1915 G. H. Deakin
Wholesale
Warehouse
1914-1912 C. W. Reynolds
Car Showroom
1912-1908 R. Sowden
Furniture
1907 J. P. Hindson
Corn Merchant
1906-1900 F. J. Atkinson
Furnisher
1900-1867 Joseph Atkinson
Furnisher

1865 Geo. Blackburn
1864-1863 Thomas Nottingham
Rose and Crown
1861 Laurence Bartie
1860-1857 Thomas Stringer
1856-1852 Edward Bradley
1850 Geo. Wray
1849-1848 Francis Rimington
1847-1845 Charles Tonge

24

1947 Mrs Richardson
1936 G. Bunting
Confectioner
1932 Parry & Co.
1930 W. Ward
1928 Parry & Co.
1927 Mrs G. hanson
Draper
1925-1924 Fred E. Harrison
1922 A. Crompton
1919 M. E. Tune
Dust Bins etc.
1914 F. W. Bent
1912-1907 E. Akeroyd
1906 F. J. Atkinson
1902 Hatton Hairdresser
1898-1892 J. W. Rodgers
1885 Mark Oldham Office
1883-1844 Joseph
Sutcliffe Office

26

1946 Keith Parker
1939-1938 N. Richmond
1937-1935 M. Dobinson
1935-1934 P. S. Bagley
1934-1923 J. Lumb
Fruiterer
1922-1882 W. Cleaver
Saddler
1882-1871 Alexander
Hildred
1870 Wm. Simpson
1868-1866 Wm. Brooks
1865 Joseph Atkinson
1864-1833 Rebecca Binns

28 (continued)

UPPER	LOWER
1868 Wm. Brooks	1868-1863 Robert Corker
1867 John Daniel	
1864-1860 Wm. Brooks Furniture Brooker	1863-1844 Thomas Summers Rope Mar
1859 Richard Smith	
1857 Wm. Hyde	
1856-1855 Wm. Dodgson	
1854-1851 Swither Bashforth Wheelwright	
1850-1844 Farrell Roark Tailor	
1842-1839 John Hodgson Shoemaker	1841 John Butterwor Weaver
1837 Swither Bashforth	1839-1836 John Pino

Number 28 seen after the 1962 alterations.

30

2001-1991 Suite Success
          Furnishings Direct
1991-1990 Barker and Wigfall TV and Electrical
1990-1985 Suite Centre
1984-1982 Super Home Furnishers
1982-1977 Barnsley Furnishing & Bedding Co.
1976-1975 Vacant
1975-1970 South Yorkshire Furnishing Co.
1969 M and L Furniture
1967-1927 Eyre Bros Garage
1915-1910 Geo. Booker Central Garage
Corn Mill
1898-1860 Jackson Bros.
1859-1854 Jackson and Watson
1852-1849 James Marsden
1848-1847 Thomas Reddish
1846-1825 Rycroft and Jackson

2001-1999 K. G. V. Public House
          Licensee Simon Linskey
Kingsleys Public House
1986-1966 **King George Hotel**
1973-1966 Albion Turner
1966-1957 Wilfred Lockyer
1957-1952 Herbert Fewkes
1952-1941 John O Mann
1941-1938 Gerard Cutts
1938-1930 Harold Wray
1930-1927 George Shaw
1927-1925 Beatrice Beaumont
1925-1922 Allan Beaumont

2001 Derelict
1991-1981 Total Filling Station
1980-1973 Petropolis Filling Station
1973 Filling Station
1962-1912 Reynolds Bros Garage

1978 Demolished
1978 Vacant
1978-1973 Builders Supplies
1968 Krazy Kuts Grocers
1963-1954 B.B.C.S. Building Supplies

Built in 1915 this was a garage until its demolition in the 1960's. During the 1970s and 80s the site was occupied by a filling station but is now vacant again as seen above.

The Ritz Cinema was built in 1937 and demolished in 1974. This and the remaining properties to Town End were replaced by Leos, now Pioneer, superstore.

2001-1991 Pioneer Superstore
1991-1982 Leos Superstore

——————————————— Demolished 1974 ———————————————

| 1974-1963 Builders Supplies | | 1974-1937 Ritz Cinema | Demolished 1960s? |

1960-1957 Dorothea Wool	1960-1953 Washington and Hawksworth Cafe	1960-1953 R. Sanderson Sweets & Tobacco		1960-1943 Borough Builders Merchants Ltd.
1950-1938 Platts and Whittaker	1952-1944 Godfrey and Kenworthy Cafe	1952-1938 R. W. Adkin Sweets & Tobacco		1942-1902 Barnsley Master Builders Co.
	1943-1944 J. Larkin Cafe			
	1943 Bennett and Platts Cafe			

These shops were opened at the same time as the cinema.

Demolished 1979

1979-1978 Rozel Motor Company

1976-1970 Stafford Antiques	1978 Coverit Two		
1969-1967 B. and G. Allen Insurance Broker	1977 Help The Aged	**Circus Yard**	Car Park
1965-1948 G. H. Wadsworth Dog Food	1976-1948 S. Kirkby Pet Shot	1961-1932 H. Speight Blacksmith	1950-c.1920 Pavillion Cinema
1938-1887 Wm. J. V. Whitham Machinist	1947-1937 G. Chew Pet Shop		c1920-1909 Olympia Skating Rink
1885-1879 Charlesworth & Son		1958-1951 E. Walton Blacksmith	1896 Thomas Fox Cab. Prop.
	1936-1935 S. R. Carr Corn Merchant	1940-1938 Mrs. E. A. Turner	1932-1911 T. Tomlin
	1934-1927 I. Cartwright Corn Merchant	1937-1920 E.. Charlesworth	
	1922-1915 S. Wheatley Hay Dealer	1929-1913 Daft and Norton Wheelwrights	
	1913 Alf Bennett	1922-1898 John Hood Builder	
		1905-1890 Geo. Birkill Furniture Remover	

The area on the south side of Peel Street between the Ritz and the Pavilion Cinema, now occupied by the Pioneer supermarket

The staff of the rink pose for a photograph.

Built as a skating rink in 1909 this became the Pavilion Cinema and was destroyed by fire in 1950.

PEEL STREET ARCADE

Peel Street Arcade leads from Peel Street to Peel Parade, which parallels Peel Street. Both were created in the rebuilding which took place in the late 1960s. See map on page 35.

7	6	3	2	1
CLOSED	2001-1996 Complete System Cadies Gym and Fitness Club	2001-1973 Dimensions Hair Salon	2001-1988 Richies Ladies Footwear	2001-1969 The Spring Box Dry Cleaners
2001-1991 Dental Health Centre	? Dimensions Health Club		Stan + Stan II Photographer	

Peel Street Arcade in 2001.

PEEL PARADE

The numbers of the units are shown where they are known.

Dog Lane	Rear of Argos	11	Rear of Jonathan James	10	Entry	9	Peel St Arcade	13	Entry
		2001-1996 Suites R us		2001-1996 Suites & Beds R us in association with Rileys		2001-1983 Treadles Wine Bar		2001-1999 Angels, Mind Body & Spirit Shop	
				1996-? House of Leather				?-? Kitchen Equipment Shop	
								?-? Ladies Boutique	

Two views of Peel Parade in 2001.

Vacant	27	33	35	37	39	Side Road
	2001 Cadlab Dental Repairs	2001-1987 Barnsley Outdoor Centre	2001-1999 Enterprise Video	2001-2000 Carpet & Bed Experience	Rear of Poundstretcher	
	2000-? The Pine Shop		1999-1987 Barnsley Outdoor Centre	Tattoo Parlour		
			1987-? Trophy Shop	Karate Club		

PITT STREET
SOUTH SIDE

2

2001-1997 Became Part of Chennels Bar
1997-1990 Blayneys Off-License
1986 Dickins Off-Licence
1982 Chennels and Armstrong
      Off-License
1980-1963 Ashley Adams
      Travel Agent
1962-1947 Central W. M. Club
1933-1931 Lonsdale Club
1930-1929 Barnsley District
      Tradesmen's Club
1928-1902 Barnsley Conservative
      Association Club

4 to 14

2001-1964 General Post Office

Jackson's Yard

Barnsley Union Relief Office

Pulled down

4

1952-1905 Barnsley Corporation Offices
1899-1880 Wm. Jackson
1880-1863 Sarah Jackson

2

1862-1841 Geo. Jackson

6

1952-1870 W. Kaye and Son
      Printers

3

1870-1863 Wm. Needham
1862 Jane Hawksworth Milliner
1859 Geo. Hirst
1857 Thomas Fletcher
1856-1855 Geo. Drake
1854-1850 Geo. Hirst
1848-1845 Elizabeth Gill
1844-1842 Joseph Tinker
1833 Wm. Tomlin

Pitt Street c1960. The lines indicate the relief road which now passes beneath Pitt Street. Reproduced from the Ordnance Survey map with the permission of Ordnance Survey on behalf of Her Majesty's Stationery Office, © Crown Copyright MC 100035068

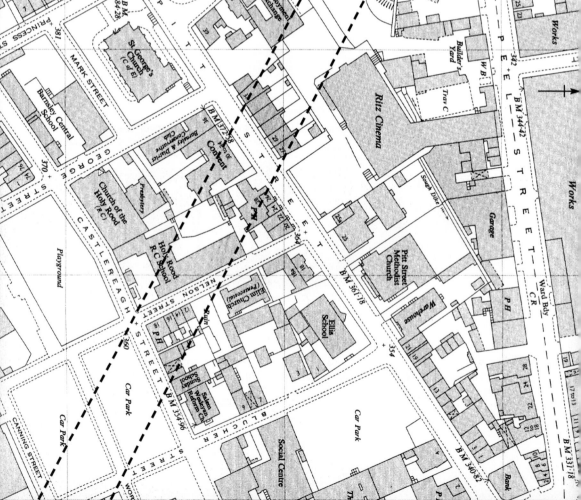

8

1952-1939 W. Kaye and
       Son Printers
1938-1926 W. Johnson
1925-1907 Johnson and
       Slater Dressmakers
1906 W. Gaimster
1905-1899 Sarah Garner
1897 Wm. Wroot
1896 Willie Linstead
1895-1890 Wm. A. Hall
1889 Geo. Brook
1885-1863 James Allen
1882 Sanderson
1881 Edward Woodhead
1880 Benjamin Harris
1879-1877 Elis Bostwick Grocer
1876-1871 Wm. Wroot Grocer

4

1870-1857 Henry Wilby Seedsman
1856 Thomas Walker
1855 Joseph Marshall
1854-1852 John Stringer
1849 Mary Fairhand
1848 Charles Ball
1847-1846 John Dennis
1845 Miss Tyas
1842 Benjamin Hinchliffe
1841-1833 Miss Schofield
1830 Wm. Milner

10

1952 Social Services
1937-1868 Wade and
       Turner Architects

10

1938-1918 A. Cousins
1915-1914 Ernest Haigh
1912 J. B. Green
1910 W. Dalton
1909-1907 A. Manslip
1906-1904 Wm. Smith
1902-1900 John Desmond
1899 M. E. Barker
1898-1897 E. M. Crossley
1896 F. Tomlin
1894-1891 S. Ellis
1885-1883 John Smith
1882 Wm. Sefton
1881-1880 James Gordon
1879-1854 Theodore Rogers
       Boot and Shoe Maker

5

1852-1850 Elizabeth Davies
1849-1845 Francis Wainford
       Grocer
1842-1840 Joseph Leadman

12

1938-1932 J. P. Round
1931-1927 J .T. Hargreaves
1926-1918 T. J. Birtles
1916-1899 Miss E. Peck
1897-1880 Henry Waters
1879-1876 Sam Croft
       Exchange Mart
1875 John Gordon
1874-1859 James Knight

6

1858-1854 James Machin
1852 Geo. Clayton
1840 Joseph McLintock

14

1938-1928 A. Wright Grocer
1927-1926 G. Hubbard Grocer
1925-1900 Charles Mycock Grocer
1899-1893 Emily Schofield Grocer
1891-1884 John Kitching
1883-1875 Thomas Twivey
1874-1864 Geo. Fox

7

1863-1852 Robert Carr Shopkeeper
1851-1850 Charles Bennett Grocer
1848-1842 Geo. Crossley Plumber
1841 Thomas Cooper

Set back from the street, in the yard at the side of this building, was the Barnsley Union Relief Office built in 1903. It replaced an earlier office in Westgate.

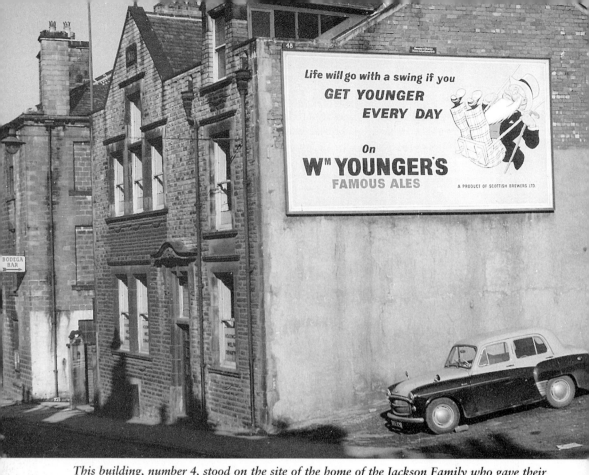

This building, number 4, stood on the site of the home of the Jackson Family who gave their name to the adjacent yard. In this yard were a number of small dwelling and workshops.

The right to carry the 'Mail' was obtained by tender. Here is a horse drawn vehicle used for this purpose by George Booker.

General Post Office built in 1964.

...l 1939 at the corner of Blucher
... Castlereagh Street was the

...on Inn

...9-1934 Alfred Jackson

...4-1933 John Cawthorne

...3-1919 Eliz. A. Leatham

...9-1900 John Leatham

...0-1884 Thomas Leatham

...4-1880 John Leatham

...0-1879 Sarah A. Nixon

...9-1878 Wm. Nixon

...8-1874 John Butler

...4-1873 R. Goodworth

...2-1860 Benjamin Goodison

...9-1844 Wm. Wilkinson

2001-1967 Y. M. C. A.
1963-1815 National School

Numbers 6 to 16 are shops in the frontage of the YMCA building

6	8	10	12	14	16
2001-1988 Barnsley Bookshop		2001-1988 Jax Music	2001-1995 A to Z Insurance	2001-1990 Kutz and Co Hair Salon	2001-1999 Zenana Ladies Fashion
1988-1968 Ken Ellis Tailor	1988-1975 Barnsley Bookshop	1987-1967 Field Sports Supplies	1995-1976 Health in the Community	?-1967 Janet Hair Fashion	1999-1990 Ellis Fashion
	1975-1970 Pollyanna		?-1974 Easiphit Homeplan		
	1970-1968 John Cooke Outfitters		1974-1970 Field Sports Supplies		
			1970-1968 Motor Transport Brokers		

Salem Chapel stands at the corner of Blucher Street and Castlereagh Street. It was built in 1825 and has been used by the Wesleyan Reform Union since 1857.

In 1967 the YMCA was built on the site of the National School. The frontage included the shops shown below.

The National School, endowed by G. Ellis and sometimes known as the Ellis School, was buuilt in 1815. It was pulled down in 1963 and replaced by the YMCA building.

Opposite to Salem Chapel was Blucher Street Chapel which was built by the Wesleyan Protestant Methodist in 1829. John Whitworth was the architect. A new front was erected in 1901. After it had ceased to be a place of worship, in 1958, it was used by the Barnsley British Cooperative Society.

18 MANSE CHAMBERS

First Floor

2001-1999 Patricia Kril
Physiotherapist
2001-1986 Dugmore Dental Practice
1986-1982 Shepherd Dental Practice
1982-1973 H. Leigh Dental Surgeon

Ground Floor

2001-1989 House of
Beauty

1973-1953 H. Leigh, Dental Surgeon
1958-1926 W. Smith, Chiropodist
1960-1936 A. Dixon, Estate Agent
1951-1923 Sugden and Riley, Dentists
1973-1948 Barnsley School of Motoring
1922-1921 Leonard W. Dickens
1920-1919 James L. Smith
1918 J. Ellis
1914 M. L. Camburn
1910-1909 A. Bourne
1908-1906 W. D. L. Slack
1904-1903 G. J. Brett
1901 Alfred Kent
1898 James Finch
1896 Edward S. Stocks
1895 E. S. Banham
1894-1892 Thomas Haslam
1891-1888 Walter G. Hall
1886-1884 Thomas Raspass
1882 E. C. Haine
1880-1878 W. Parsonson
1877 Phillip Fowler
1874 Thomas Thompson
1871 Wm. Slater
1866 W. J. Binder

1852 J. Osbourne	1852-1850 Alice Spencer
1850-1848 S. Simmons	1849-1847 John M. Keir
1847 Capp	1846-1841 Miss Gelder
1844 S. R. Taylor	
1841 Brown	

18A to rear of 18

2001-1996 Life Pregnancy
Care Centre

Nelson Street

Shortened when relief road built.

In Nelson Street was the

Eagle Inn

1931-1928 Emma Wordsworth
1928-1922 Wm. Wordsworth
1922-1912 Thomas Bower
1912-1909 John Hornby
1909-1908 Thomas Shaw
1908-1899 Frank Shaw
1899-1897 James Hamer
1897-1988 James Wilkinson
1888-1881 John Walshaw
1881-1880 Henry Taylor
1880-1877 C. O'Donoghue
1877- James Steel
1877-1872 James Simmons
1872-1862 Thomas Simmons

Demolished for bridge over relief road

Row of cottages
(Linen) built 1860,
number 20 to 26,
which replaced a
row of six cottages
known as Malton
Place

Vine Tavern

?-1973 Wm. Varley
1973-1967 Thomas C. Ellis
1967-1960 Wm. H. Lawton
1960-1952 Rupert Kenworthy
1952-1946 Harold Jones
1946-1941 Joseph H. Armitage
1941-1933 Harold Stringer
1933-1926 Thomas Sanderson
1926-1922 Harry Newrick
1922-1912 Charles Foster
1912-1896 John Harrison
1896-1894 Edward Worthington
1894-1889 George Belleini
1889-1884 John T. Newsum
1884-1875 Christopher Pryor
1875 Charles Regan
1875-1868 Matha Sykes
1868-1866 Matthew Sykes
1865-1864 Jane E. Coward
1863-1862 Thomas Coward
1861-1860 George S. Coles
1859- Isaac Dennis
1857-1849 Wm. Oxley
1848-1845 Thomas White
1844-1842 Ann Bennett
1841-1839 Joseph Bennett
1837-1835 James McClellan
1833 Widow Hepworth
1830 Ellis Wade

Manse Chambers in 2000, and the YMCA building.

The Manse Chambers was unitl 1922 the home of nonconformist ministers. Since then it has been used as offices. Shown here in 1960 with the National School beyond.

These cottages, numbers 20 to 26, had stone steps up to a raised doorway and a low window at street level.

The Vine Tavern in 1960.

On the left is the foreshortened Nelson Street and beyond is the bridge over the relief road, replacing the Vine Tavern and the Convent.

——— Demolished for bridge over relief road ———

1980-1949 Convent of The Sisters of Mercy

1949-1900 Convent of the Sisters of Mercy

36
2001-1927 Barnsley Conservative Association
1922 T. C. Walsh
1921-1915 J. Sheridan
1914-1900 H. Knowles
1899-1898 G. J. Kell
1897-1886 Septimus Green
1885-1879 Henry Piggott
1874-1869 Henry Harvey

George Street

30
1899-1885 Henry Knowles
1883-1877 Jeremiah Scott
1874-1865 Wm. T. Y. Scott

32
1897-1880 Thomas B. Lowrance
1879-1864 Henry Harvey

34
1949-1915 E. Sheridan
1914-1900 H. Knowles
1899- E. W. Woodhead
1898-1891 James Ellan
1890-1887 Thomas White
1886-1872 Fanny Richardson

14
1863-1847 S. B. Jackson
1846-1833 Henry Richardson

15
1863-1861 John Twibell
1860 Matthias Watts
1857-1854 David Byrd
1852-1846 Rev. E. Maxwell
1845-1833 Ann Haxworth

16
1871-1865 John T. Pigott
1860-1853 Sarah Wilson
1852-1844 Thomas Wilson
1841-1837 Edward Parker
1833 William Mawer

17
1868-1841 Wm. Harvey
1833 Joseph Naylor

These early nineteenth century houses were the homes of prominent citizens. In the twentieth century three of them became a convent. The one on the right is still used by the Conservative Association and is the only part now standing, as seen in the smaller picture.

PITT STREET

NORTH SIDE

7

2001- Jalsa Tandoori
Restaurant & Takeaway
1990 Pipasha Tandoori Restaurant
1982 Trattoria Venezia Restaurant
1978-1974 Vacant
1973-1966 Grill Room
1965-1962 Hong Kong Restaurant
1961-1957 M. Lowrance & Son
Ironmongers
1956-1934 Fred Robinson
1933-1902 Martin Robinson
1900 Florence Atkinson
1899-1898 Mary Higgins
1897-1896 S. Rooke
1895-1887 Wm. Wroot
1886 Charles Holmes
1885-1880 Frederick Sanderson
Carting & Removals
1879 John Charlesworth
1878-1873 Benjamin Smith
Veterinary Surgeon
1872-1870 George Bonson

3

Farriers Arms
1868-1867 John Stone
1866 George Bonson
1865 Wm. Stringer
1864-1863 Thomas Horne
1862-1861 Robert Sampson
1860 Nancy Bradley
1859-1840 Thomas Liddall Farmer

5

2001- Empty
2000-1996 L. A. Steel
Solicitiors
1993-1989 William H. Brown
Estate Agent/Surveyors
1989-1984 Stanilands/ W.H. Brown
Estate Agents/Surveyors
1984- F. E. Pattison Estate Agent
1973-1960 E. E. Peterson
Estate Agents
1959-1955 H .E. Leigh
Dental Surgeon
1954 E. Banks
1953-1882 Copes Servants
Registry Office
1881 Henry Powell
1880-1876 Elizabeth Mackie
1875-1873 John B. Freeman
1870-1863 Edward Abson
1862-1861 Peter Day
1860-1859 Edward Abson
1858 Ann Tetley
1857 Charles Thawley
1856 Timothy Exley
1855-1854 Wm. Green

3

2001-1997 Spoilt For Choice
Ladies Fashions
1996-1995 Catalogue Shop
1994-1953 Geoffrey Barnard
Hi-Fi Equipment
1953-1952 J. B. Studio
1951-1950 Norwood &
Perrin Opticians
1949-1899 J. Wheatley
Tailor
1898 Zillah Sharrott
1897-1896 R. Sewell
1895 Joseph Lawton
1894-1891 Robert Carr
1890-1877 Mary Horne
1876-1875 John A. Crawshaw
1874 John P. Freeman

1

2001-1989 London Scottish Finance
1988-1974 Refuge Lending Society
1973-1898 Cleveland Dairy
1897 J. W. Lambe
1896-1887 Septimus Green
1886 C. Hopkinson
1885-1883 Herbert Crawshaw
1882-1880 Walter Ogley
1878-1875 Robert Ennis
1874 John A. Crawshaw

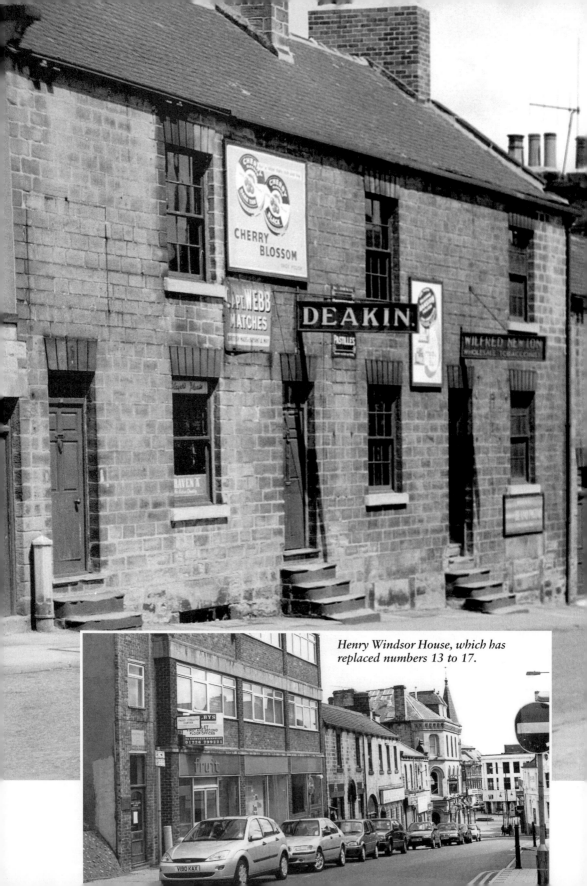

Henry Windsor House, which has replaced numbers 13 to 17.

When first built this was a row of private houses but with the passing of time they became shops, offices and warehouses. Seen here in the 1950s.

13
HENRY WINDSOR HOUSE

GROUND FLOOR	FIRST FLOOR
2001-2000 Fruits Hair Design	2001 Empty
1999-1995 Welcome Windows Showroom	2001-2000 Gibson Booth Paget Coggins Chartered Accountants
? Carpet Showroom	2000-1985 Paget Coggins, Carter Chartered Accountants

Rebuilt as No. 13

11/9
2001-2000 The Room Hair Salon

Fruits Hair Design

———— Demolished 1973 ————

17

1960-1927 C. H. Deakin Wholesale Tobacconist
1926-1918 F. A. Dixon
1915-1912 S. Cawthorne
1911 A. Johnson
1910 J. Brinton
1908-1907 R. Snowden
1906-1901 T. Dickinson Apartments
1900 E. Hill
1899 Hy. Ed. South
1897-1871 Edward Jeffrey Doctor

32

1870-1864 Thomas Ellison
1865-1864 W. F. H. Smith
1863-1861 Anthony Edson
1860 Michael Clayton
1859-1857 James Ellam
1856 Benjamin G. Wilson
1855-1854 Alfred Rowley
1852-1849 George James
1848 Robert R. Raywood
1847 Elizabeth Kenn
1845-1840 Mrs Dewar
1839-1833 Mrs. Armitage
1830 C. H. Pickles
1825 B. Coldwell

15

1960-1927 C. H. Deakin Wholesale Tobacconist
1926-1921 W. Cherryholme
1920-1893 John Kitching Carting Agent
1892 W. A. S. Hollingworth
1891-1889 T. F. Dickinson
1888 Tom Fenton
1887-1882 Emily Mason
1879 E. Cook
1877-1873 Jabez Stephenson

33

1872 Tinker
1871-1869 Thomas Pepper
1868-1854 Sarah Huntington
1852 Thomas Frudd
1850 Thomas King
1849-1846 John Robinson
1845 Footitt
1844-1835 Anne Barber
1833 Wm. Gunyon
1833 Brown & Hutton

13

1958-1932 W. Newton Wholesale Tobacconist
1930-1926 L. Goodworth
1926-1915 E. J. White
1914-1910 Wm. Peacock
1909-1906 A. Fox
1905-1899 Elizabeth Dale
1898-1895 Frederick Crow
1893 W. Wood
1892-1830 Sarah Green

34

11

1960-1954 S. Jones
1953-1945 F. Lee
1938-1927 T. Lyman
1926-1903 E. Oates
1902-1900 Moritz Lieske
1899 John Desmond
1898 M. H. Brown
1897-1896 A. Chadwick
1895 Geo. Barrett
1894 F. Tomlin
1893-1891 Thomas Pryor
1890 W. Bennett
1889-1887 J. Bushby
1886 Widow Cheatham
1883-1882 Jane Burdett
1880 Amos Wike
1877 Wm. Tasker
1874-1870 Bridget Liddall

9

1961-1949 G. Lane
1948 M. Thornton
1947-1945 E. Tattingham
1938 F. Lee
1933-1902 Mark Robinson
1900-1899 James Preston
1898-1895 Annie Wilkinson
1894 T. Oates
1893 A. Axon
1892-1889 Edward Brown
1887 James Chambers
1886 Geo. Washbrook
1883-1882 Edward Wood
1880 John Knowles
1877-1875 Margaret Ross
1874 Charles Matthews
1872-1871 Margaret Ross
1870-1864 Hannah Huntley Milliner
1860 Joseph Blackshaw

A group of people gathered outside the Temperance Hall. The white aprons of the women and the white collars of the boys should be noted.

Demolished 1974

21

1973-1955 E. T. Haywood
　　　　　Newsagent
1954 D. Haggs
1952-1950 R. Williams
1950-1948 A. E. Murphy
1948-1935 W. J. Savage
1935-1930 T. W. Taylor
1929-1928 F. Charlton
1927-1919 D. J. Curtis
1918 Dora Brailsford
1917 Cyril Hall
1916 C. E. Timewell
1915-1907 John Hall Tailor
1905 Robert Bailey Stationer
1903 A. Cleave Tobacconist
1902-1898 Lucy Smith
　　　　　Servant's Registry
　　　　　Office
1897-1883 Benjamin Pogson
1881 Sydney Smith
1880-1871 Wm. Bramald
　　　　　Furniture Maker

30

1870 Benjamin Drake
1869 Murray
1868-1864 Anthony Edson
1863 James Brown
1861-1859 Thomas Cowan
　　　　　Draper
1858-1857 Mark Hill
1856-1855 Geo. Hirst
1852-1851 Joseph McLintock
1850 John Cope
1849 John Blackhouse
1848-1847 John Hattersley
1845-1837 Wm. Green Cabinet
　　　　　Maker Auctioneer

19

1973-1965 G. Williams Cafe
1964 Wm. Oscroft Cafe
1963-1961 Hugh Brady Cafe
1960-1949 E. Short Cafe
1948-1943 G. Bishop
1937 Jack Hayes
1933-1926 A. Fletcher
1925-1893 Mary Burrows
1892-1862 Mary Hill

31

1860 Robert Mitchell
1859 Joseph Tinker
1857 Martin Wright
1856 John Braime
1855 Timothy Oxley
1852-1850 James Marsden
1848-1846 David Bennett
1845-1833 Thomas Fox Traveller

These two stone built shops, built as houses early in the nineteenth century, still retained a feeling of that period in the 1960s.

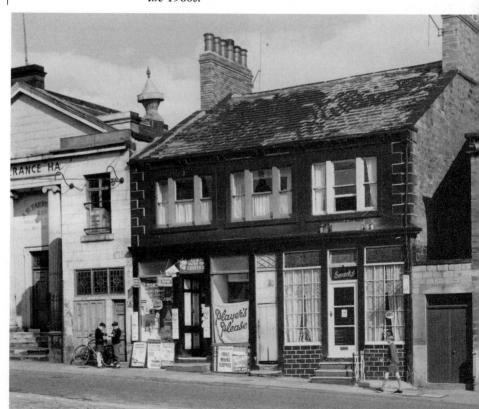

Demolished c1980

25

1973-1950 J. Lodge & Son Warehouse

1939-1937 H. Lewis & Son Sale Room

1936-1906 E .W. Blackburne
        House and Surgery

1905-1861 John Blackburne

1860 John E. Twibell

1857 Samuel King

1856-1844 Geo. H. Smith

1842-1837 Geo. H. Smith

    1841 Mrs Wood

    1839 Mrs Guest

    1838-1837 Rev. J. Armitage

    1833-1825 Miss Hindles

1878-1865 Haxworth Carnley
       & Sample Warehouse

1860 John Whitworth

1856-1848 Geo. H. Smith
       Linen Warehouse

1842 Smith & Parkinson

1840 Wm. Harvey

2001-1987 Rebuilt Chapel

Demolished 1984

Wesleyan Chapel

Foundation stone laid by
Thomas Cope 1845
Opened 1846

Built 1836 Temperance Hall

First Floor:

2001 Closed

1999-1997 Radical & Liberal Club

Basement:

2001-1995 Premier Fitness Studio

1995-1993 Ultrafit Gym

Ground Floor:

2001-1993 Panama Joes Licencee - Joanne Roberts

1992 alterred and extended

c1990-1952 J. W. Farnsworth Warehouse

1946 Central School of Dancing

1928-1923 Cosy Picture House

1909 Royal Canadian Pictures

1905 J. Ray School

1897-1880 Temperance Society

1873-1869 Benjamin Hague

1868-1848 Thomas Dale

1847-1836 Oddfellows Hall (Thomas Batty)

In 1837 Thomas Towers held a license which was refused
1838 but in 1839 Thomas Wheatley held a license

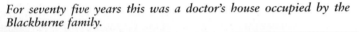

*For seventy five years this was a doctor's house occupied by the
Blackburne family.*

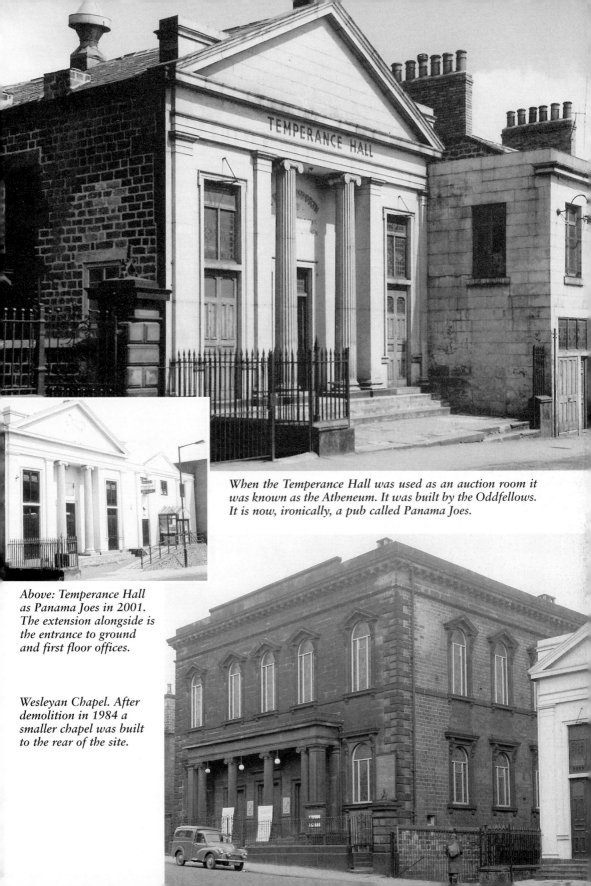

When the Temperance Hall was used as an auction room it was known as the Atheneum. It was built by the Oddfellows. It is now, ironically, a pub called Panama Joes.

Above: Temperance Hall as Panama Joes in 2001. The extension alongside is the entrance to ground and first floor offices.

Wesleyan Chapel. After demolition in 1984 a smaller chapel was built to the rear of the site.

Demolished 1973

Bore Spring Mill (Demolished 1930s)

39

1972-1920 Barnsley Corporation Offices

1912-1876 Henry Wade

1875-1852 Benjamin Robinson School

1851-1841 Wm. Laycock

1840-1837 Wm. Maitland

1835-1825 John Taylor

37-27

St. George's Place

Six house numbers 27 to 37

Pulled down in 1973

1931-1930 S. Fletcher & Son

1929-1853 Richardson, Tee & Rycroft Linen Works

1851-1840 Henry Richardson

1846-1840 Pigott and Newton Linen Mill

1838 Mason & Richardson

1837-1835 James Cocker

1830-1825 Ward & Cocker

The new Methodist Church built on the site of the demolished chapel. In 2001 this was to be closed and amalgamated with a new Methodist Chapel on Huddersfield Road.

No. 39. A school and a house for the first part of its life, this building had been used as offices since 1920 by Barnsley Corporation.

Saint George's Place had one of the most pleasing facades of any row of houses in Barnsley.

Saint George's Church, viewed from the south side, was demolished in the 1980s.

The site of Saint George's Church, viewed from the north side – Pitt Street, in 2001.

ALHAMBRA CENTRE
LOWER (CHEAPSIDE) LEVEL

1
2001-2000 Claires Accessories
2000-1995 Electronics Boutique
1995-1994 Futurezone
1994-1993 Benetton

2
2001-1998 Ciro Citterio
1998-1995 Sweater Shop
1995-1991 Athena

3
2001-1994 Allsports
1994-1993 G. H. W. Tradehouse
1993-1992 Prima Sports

4
2001-1993 Barnsley Building Society

5
2001-1992 Roseby's

6
2001-1998 Melody

7
2001-1993 Partners The Stationers

8/9
2001-1992 Woolworths

10
2001-1992 Select

11
2001-1993 Massarellas Coffee Shop

12
2001-2000 Name change to Outdoor Venture
2000-1998 Famous Army Stores
1997-1994 Shoe Express

13
2001-1998 The Officers Club
1998-1993 Fosters Menswear
1993-1992 Music for You

14/15
2001-1992 Bon Marche

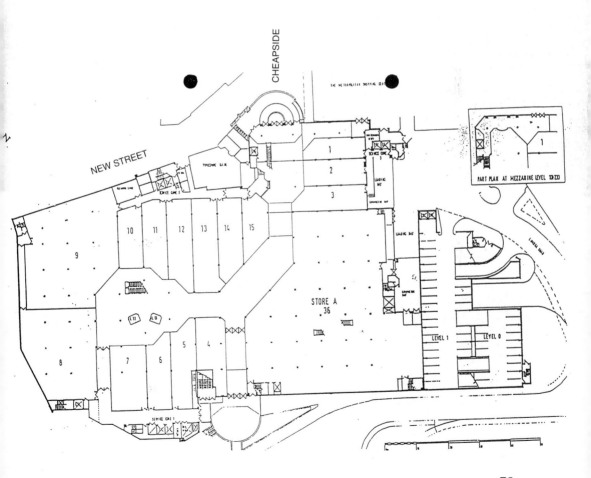

UPPER (NEW STREET) LEVEL

16	16B	17	17A	18/19	20	21
2001-1999 Reds in Town 1998-1993 Fox's Music	2001-1998 Empty. Formed after split of unit 38	2001-1999 Olivers Timpson 1999-1995 Paris Shoes	2001-1995 Stitch Express	2001-1994 NEXT	2001-1999 Gift Tree 1999-1998 Tough Terrain	2001-1999 Hair Express 1999-1998 Reds in Town 1998-1995 Not Just Books 1995-1994 Sell Off

22-25
— 2001-1998 Wilkinson —

22	23	24	25	26/27	28/29	30	31/32
1998-1993 Wilkinson	1998-1997 Shopmobility 1995-1992 Letting Suite	1998-1993 Empty	1998-1993 Empty	2001-1995 Mothercare	2001-1999 M. V. C.	2001-1992 Sugg Sport	2001-1998 Peacocks

33	34	35	35A	36 Upper	36 Lower	37	Upper Ma Lottery Ki
2001-1999 Betty Blue 1998-1997 Tough Terrain 1995-1994 EGS Records	2001-2000 Favourites 2000-1999 Gadgets & Cards 1998-1997 Milaps 1997-1994 Especially Yours	2001-1999 KAR 1999-1997 London Fashion 1995-1993 Bookscene	2001-1994 Clever Cobbler	2001-2000 T. K. Maxx now unit 38 upper mall 1999-1998 Living 1998-1991 Living	2001-2000 Primark	2001-1994 Vacant 1994-1992 Poppy's Tearooms	2001-1996

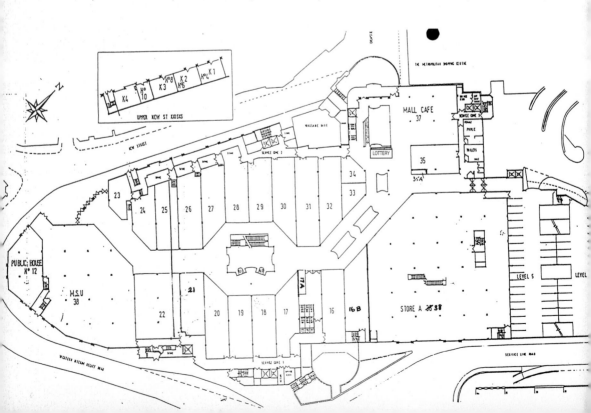

NEW STREET

SOUTH SIDE

2001-1978 Yorkshire Bank

1978 Under Construction for Yorkshire Bank

1977 Demolished

1976 Vacant

Kiosk 1

(NB: The 'Kiosks' are four shops, part of the Alhambra Centre, facing onto New Street)

2001-1996 Uppercrust II Sandwich Bar

1989 January Demolished for Alhambra Centre

2

1973-1909 J. Hadwen & Sons Tailors

1908-1898 Hadley Hudson Tailor

1897 Foster Bros. Footwear

1896 J. H. Bailey

Re-built

1893-1897 Derricks Baskets-Toys
(Richard Holden)

1886-1883 Jabez Wheatley Tailor

1882 Wm. Wood

1881-1875 Charles Firth Fancy Goods

1874-1871 Martha Ash Fancy Goods

Shamrock Inn

1869-1867 Sarah Leary

1866-1863 John Leary

Lord Raglan Inn

1860- Charles Sedgwick

4

1973-1915 J. Hadwen & Sons Tailors

1914-1895 Tom Scarbrough Draper

1893-1891 John Payne

1890 H. Wallace

1888-1883 Tom Brown Stationer

1882-1880 James Eaton

1879-1841 James Blackshaw hairdresser

6

1988-1972 Greens Telecom

1972-1970 Empty

1969-1959 Dobsons Radio

1958-1947 Harold Senior

1946-1913 Fletcher and Frankland Drapers

1912-1899 Mrs A. Crummack Hosier

1898-1895 Taylors Drug Store

1890-1887 Herbert Crook

1886-1883 C. O. Donoghue

1882-1881 Ann Bray

1880 Henry Jagger

Map of New Street c1960. The lines show the outline of the Alhambra Centre and the Westway relief road.

Reproduced from the Ordnance Survey map with the permission of Ordnance Survey on behalf of Her Majesty's Stationery Office, © Crown Copyright MC 100035068

New Street today, with the Alhambra Centre along the left hand side.

The passage way between Dobsons and the Maypole is of interest as it may mark the original right of way onto what was Oxley' Yard. Photographed in 1960

It is easy to see why in early records the corner shop was sometimes considered to be in New Street and at other times in Sheffield Road. Danish Dairy Farmers occupied the site between 1889 and 1917.

Kiosk 2	Kiosk 3
2001-2000 Advance Dry Cleaners	2000 Empty

────────── January 1989 Demolished for Alhambra Centre ──────────

OXLEYS YARD

White Lion

1869 Geo. Blackburn
1868 Charles Nixon
1867 Malachi Devany
1866 Geo. Blackburn
1865-1856 James Clough Pawnbroker
1855-1854 T. Brook Co.

8

1988-1985 The Private Shop (Sex shop)
1985-1982 Vacant
1982-1977 Bewildered Ladies Wear
1977-1973 Nepentha D Ladies Wear
1973-1969 Empty
1969-1962 Red Arrow Radio Rentals
1960-1897 Maypole Diary Co.
1896 J. Lumb
Rebuilt
1893-1868 Ann Bray

109

1867-1852 W. Sedgwick Confectioner
1851-1849 Hannah Tyne
1848-1847 Felix McGee
1846-1845 Mark Rose
1844-1841 John Campbell Weaver

10

1988-1982 Photo Centre
1982-1978 Photomart
1978-1973 Cutlers Photo Dealers
1973-1970 Empty
1969-1957 Radio Rentals
1956-1955 Blackshaw Tailor
1954-1950 Rita Childrens Outfitter
1949 R. Ibberson
1947-1940 H. S. Stear
1939-1914 Argentine Meat Co.
1913-1911 J. Nelson & Son Butchers
1909-1906 E. Pickles Dining Room
1905-1902 C. F. Clayton Albany Dining Room
1901-1899 Clays Bazaar
1898-1896 Peter Oldfield
Rebuilt
1893-1892 S. Threlfall
1891-1890 K. Riley
1889-1887 C. O'Donoghue
1886-1885 Mary A. Pomfret
1883-1841 Joseph Fogg Shoemaker

108

12

1988-1986 Vacant
1985-1978 ART Wallpaper & Paint
1978-1956 Morris Wallpapers
1955-1946 Shaw and Co. Furnishers
1945-1944 Murphy Furniture
1942-1934 R. Mitchell Furniture
1933-1909 Atkinson & Sons Furnishers
1908-1895 Jesse Hepworth Ladies Outfitters
Rebuilt
1893-1891 I. Pryor Watchmaker
1890-1886 Lewis Woolas Hairdresser
1884 J. Wilson
1883- J. Priestley
1882 David Haywood

108

1881 Emmanuel Prince
1880 Walter Parkin
1879-1873 James Heaton
1872 Joshua Ward

107

1871 J. Silverwood
1870-1844 Ruth Wike Pawnbroker

14

1988-1986 N.S.P.C.C. Charity Shop
1986-1985 Homecharm Wallpaper & Paint
1985-1976 P. J. Textiles
1976-1974 Empty
1974-1972 Windsor Betting Shop
1970-1971 Telefusion
1969-1946 Spiers Fancy Goods
1942-1934 Lloyds Northern Counties Wireless Dealers
1933-1928 Stylo Boot Co.
1927-1917 Stylo and Scott Clothiers
1916-1905 Jackson Store Ltd Furnishers
1902-1897 Mrs Hy. Shaw Milliner
1896 T. Brown
Rebuilt
1893 W. Train
1892-1891 Wm. Forester
1890-1825 Wm. S. Wike
(Ruth)

106

16

1988-1986 Vacant
1985-1976 P & J Textiles
1982-1962 Smith Cleaners
1961-1959 Argo Foods
1958-1951 D. and E. M. Bielby Tobacconists
1950-1910 S. W. Webster Tobacconists
1909-1903 Bon Marche Fruit Dealer
1902-1901 Walter Merry Tailor
1900-1897 Walter Swaine Tailor

Rebuilt

16

1893-1887 Geo. Hirst
1886-1884 L. Anderson
1880 Walter Wike
1879 James Eaton
1878 F. Ogley
1877 Wm. Ellison
1876 Wm. Hearn
1875-1873 Charles Tomlinson
1872-1871 John Aspinall Brush Maker

105

1870-1868 Geo. Bray
1867-1861 John Dunstan
1860-1854 Dominic Clary Shoemaker

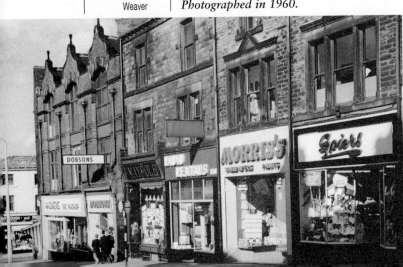

Although these shops were built at the same time in 1894, they show an interesting variation in treatment. Photographed in 1960.

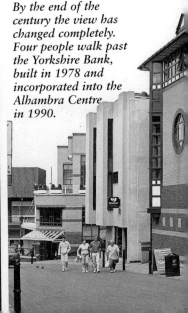

By the end of the century the view has changed completely. Four people walk past the Yorkshire Bank, built in 1978 and incorporated into the Alhambra Centre in 1990.

18

1988-1986 Vacant
1985-1976 P & J Textiles
1977-1972 Oxfam shop
1972-1967 Empty
1967-1961 Morrisons
    Fashions
1960 Alan Breck Radio
1959-1958 Electric Washer
    Services
1957-1896 F. Race Footwear

20

1989-1978 Oxfam
    Charity Shop
1978 Vacant
1978-1972 B.B.C.S. World Travel
    Travel Agents
1971-1928 B.B.C.S, Butchers
1924 B.B.C.S. Wireless Dept.
1923-1917 H. Wigfall Sons
    Cycles
1915 H. Holden
1914-1897 A. Edson
    Dyers & Cleaners

22

1989-1977 Stuart Russell Florist
1973-1972 BBCS Funeral Services
1971-1963 B.B.C.S. Electric Goods
1962-1928 B.B.C.S. Confectioners
1920 B.B.C.S. Blouse Shop
1919-1913 J. H. Bailey
1912-1905 F. Potter Hosier
1902-1901 Herbert Marshall
    General Dealer
1900-1899 Henry Shaw
1898 Martin Robinson
1897 R. Sampson

24

1989-1971 B.B.C.S. Funeral Services
1971-1967 B.B.C.S. Ironmongers Dept.
1966-1920 B.B.C.S. Furnishing Dept.
1919-1899 J. H. Bailey Furnishing

Rebuilt

1893-1881 Wm Bramley
    Ice Cream Dir
1880-1877 Robt Priestley
1875 Wm Legg
1874-1869 Uriah Brettonner
    Tailor

100

1868-1856 Joseph Dennis
Hairdresser
1852 Ed Bradley
1851-1848 Francis Butler
1846 Josiah Jobling
1845-1844 John Barlow
1842-1841 Wm Fox
1839 Wm May
1836-1833 Wm Goodworth

1892-1884 Tom Brown
Oyster Bar
1883-1882 John Green
1881 Tom Stenton
1880 Saul Mackey
1877-1835 John Ogden
    House &
    Bakehouse

99

(Thomas)

(John)

uilt

3-1881 Robert Priestly
0-1878 Elizabeth
    Blackshaw
7 Wm. Lotherington
6 Charles Tomlinson
5-1868 Alfred Flood
    Hairdresser

4

7-1862 John Dunstan
1 John McDoul
0 Joseph Flood
9-1825 John Dunstan
    Grocer

Rebuilt
20

1893-1891 F. Race
1890-1881 Wm. Threlfall
1880-1878 Samuel Clayton
1877-1875 Thomas Hodgson
1874 Crowther and McKenny

103

1871-1869 A. N. Gilderdale
    Hairdresser
1868 Wm. Fearn
1867-1855 Joseph Exley
    Rag Merchant
1854-1848 Jabez McLintock
    Rag Merchant
1846-1844 Wm. Fox
1842 Joseph Crabtree
1839 Thomas Towers
1837 John Brooksbank

Rebuilt
22

1894-1891 Joseph H. Bailey
1874-1825 Uriah Brettoner

102

(Ruth)

(John)

Rebuilt
24

1894-1875 Joseph H. Bailey
1890-1846 Jane Rose
    Greengrocer

(Mark)

101

1854-1844 John Barlow
1842-1841 Wm. Fox Bacon
    Factor
1839 Wm. May
1836-1833 Wm. Goodworth

These smart looking substantial shops contrast with their predecessors depicted on page 87.

January 1989 Demolished for Alhambra Centre

26
1988-1980 Waring Gillow
           Furniture/Carpets
1980-1960 John Peters Furniture
1959-1871 John Guest Ltd.
           Clothiers & Pawn Brokers

98
1870 George Lodge
1869-1867 John Wilcock and Son
1866-1861 Geo. Crookes Grocer
1860-1850 Vincent Housley Grocer
1849 Joseph Winter
1848-1847 Geo. Jackson Flour Dealer
1846-1839 Rycroft and Co.

Baker Street
In Baker Street was the
Old Pavillion
1986 Name changed from
        Industry Inn
Industry Inn
1973-1965 Ronald Langley
1965-1952 Wm. Hodgson
1952-1945 Elizabeth Green
1945-1935 Geo. Green
1935 Fred Hather
1935-1930 John N. Hudson
1930-1913 Henry Jackson
1913-1895 Samuel Jackson
1895-1889 Wm. J. Guilar
1889-1874 Geo. Wilkinson
1873-1871 John Haywood
1870 Geo. Wilkinson
1869 Joseph Scales
1868-1866 Joseph Addy
1865 Richard McCann

Also in Baker Street were
The **Elephant and Castle**
1869-1860 George Farrow and
The **Royal Arms** 1869-1860 Wm. Hill and
The **Spotted Cow** 1840 Geo. Haywood

The front portion of this building was a clothing and footwear store. The entrance to the pledge office was at the side in Baker Street.

Numbers 24 and 26 in 1960. During repairs in the 1950s the name J. H. Bailey was exposed to be covered again by The Barnsley British Co-operative Society Limited.

Tom Brown's Oyster Bar seems somewhate incongruous amongst such poor property. These properties were replaced by numbers 22 and 24 at the end of the nineteenth century.

The interior of the B.B.C.S. Wireless Shop which must bring back memories to those whose boyhood coincided with the 'Crystal Set' years.

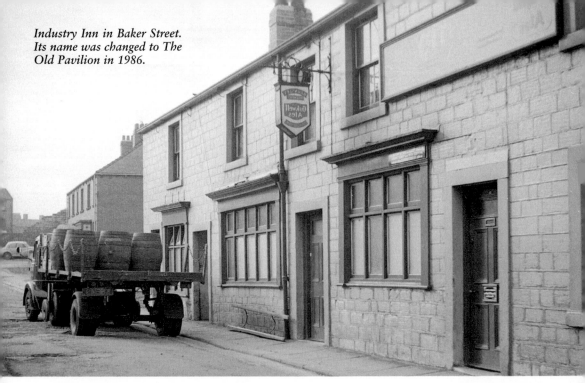

Industry Inn in Baker Street. Its name was changed to The Old Pavilion in 1986.

The Elephant Hotel sign was not distinct because the previous name was showing through. It was known as the Neptune until 1933.

28/30

1988-1978 Don Valley Sports
1978-1955 Crown Wallpapers
1955-1949 Cadman Bailey House Furniture

28

1948-1941 G. M. Wordworth
1940 Northern Wine Stores
1937-1931 W. Markham Grocer
1929-1919 M. Threlfall Grocer
1918 Guy Pickering
1917-1913 Wm. Parnham
1912-1910 Sarah Harris
1909-1876 Sarah Riley Grocer
1875-1871 Alfred Flood Hairdresser
1870-1859 Wm. Gamlins

30

1948-1947 D. M. Senior
1946-1945 A. C. Wormald
1943 C. P. Carney
1940-1937 Lawrences Ltd.
1935-1934 Mrs L. Bacon Butcher
1933-1876 H. Smith Pork Butcher
1875-1870 Hannah Peckett Boot-Shoe Broker

97

1857-1851 Geo. Corlridge
1850 Joseph Graham
1849 Joseph Mitchell
1848 Geo. Goodair
1846-1841 Thomas Dailey

96

1869-1864 John Hebden
1863 Wm. Malkin
1862-1856 Geo. Allen
1855-1852 Hy. Wilby
1851-1849 Thomas Firth
1848 Robt. Widdop
1847 Thomas Firth
1846-1844 Richard Widdop

32

1988-1986 M&V Electrical
1986 Vacant
1985-1973 Trident Discount Centre
1971-1963 Farrards Store
Elephant Hotel
1961-1959 Geo. Senior
1959-1958 Fred Stott
1957 Charles Gamewell
-1957 Wilfred Armitage
1957-1956 Robert Poskitt
1956-1954 Wm. Tease
1954 Charles King
1954-1953 Edmund Hill
1953-1952 Walter Smith
1952-1951 John R. Stanyon
1951-1938 Fred Stott

32/34

1938-1937 Charles Gamewell
1937-1936 Joseph M. Joyce
1936- Louie Dransfield
1936-1935 Maurice G. O'Callagan
1935-1933 Thomas C. Haran
1933 Arthur C. Smith
Neptune Inn
1933-1929 Geo. Green
1929 Oscar Hartley
1929-1915 Geo. Hy. White
1915-1887 Fred Carr
1887-1886 Charles Bentley
1886-1876 Henry Wilkinson

1876-1865 Joseph Mitchell
1864- Ellison
1863-1861 Ann Fox
1860-1854 James Fox
1852-1851 Ann Ellison
1850-1845 Charles Ellison
1844 Wm. Thompson
1842-1841 Hy. Denton
1839-1830 James Smith
1825 John Kay
1822 Geo. Race
1818 John Schofield

1877-1872 J. Allen Tailor
1868-1865 James Thresh
1854-1841 T. Lingard

The Neptune inn between 1929 and 1915 when Geo. Hy. White was landlord.

January 1989 Demolished for Relief Road

36

1989-1981 R. & R. Prints

1981-1971 Tasker Photographic

1971-1963 E. G. Tasker
Photographs

Raywood Row closed for building of new number 36

Raywood Row | Shop pulled down Park Row widened.

1963-1948 E. G. Tasker
Photographic Dealer

1947-1939 K. Wills

1938-1934 W. Sedgwick
Wringing Machines

1933-1915 Drapery Bazaar

1914-1906 C. V. Watts Smallware

1905-1890 Hy. B. Wilson
Smallware

1889-1885 Blythe Evison
Smallware

1884-1881 J. Riley Smallware

1880-1870 Thomas Sutcliffe
Hosier

1869 Charles Woodruffe

PARK ROW

In Park Row was the Granville Inn of which little is known. Matthew Furman was landlord when the license was withdrawn in 1869.

38/40/42

1986-1985 M&V Electrical/Audio

38/40

1985-1976 The Vac Shop T.V. and Electrical

38

1976-1972 John Clarke
Personal Loans

1971 Withers Television
Centre

1970-1964 P. Watson
Sweets-Tobacco

1961-1931 Claytons
Confectioners

1930-1928 E. Walshaw

1927- Star Tailoring

1922-1920 Economy
Tailoring Co.

1916 Arthur Glassby

1915-1883 John Rhymer
Boot Maker

1880 Wm. Hall

1879-1872 Joseph Brotherton

1871-1964 Jane Baron

1863-1862 John Broadhead

1861-1859 Joseph Crossley
Grocer

1857 Geo. Hirst

1856 John Hanson

1927-1921 M. Appleton
Draper

1920-1917 S. Shearman
Dressmaker

40

1968-1920 C. Bladen
Hairdresser

1915-1905 John Rymer

1902-1890 Job Clayton

1889-1887 G. Heeley

1886 D. Hemingway

42

1982-1962 E. Sugden
Furniture

1961-1902 Claytons
Sweets-Tobacco

1901 Clarksons Brewery

1897 L. Cassigranda

COTTAGES AND COURT

photographic equipment   TASKER   TASK

In the constuction of this old shop were several oak beams in the main structure, the end of one can be seen in the side wall. In 1963 this building and the hotel to the left were replaced with a new building to accommodate a proposed new road. Mr Tasker relocated in the new building which was itself demolished in 1989.

January 1989 Demolished for Relief Road

44/46/48
1986-1976 The Vac Shop

44
1976-1951 H. Wordsworth Dog Meat
1936-1931 S. Brook Grocer
1930 L. Rusby
1927-1926 C. Coates Dining Room
1918 G. White Butcher
1915 Walter Ogden
1913-1912 Hy. Wright Butcher
1911 B. Stow
1910 Mary Wright
1909-1903 Henry McCoy Grocer
1902 L. Newton Watchmaker

46
1976-1971 The Vac Shop
1968-1959 A. E. Littlewood Chiropodist
1958-1948 J. R. Cherry Chiropodist
1936-1929 P. Smith Butcher
1928-1927 H. Hardy Fried Fish
1922-1914 L. Cassigranda Fried Fish
1913-1909 Wilfred Sellers
1908-1906 James W. Heeley

48
1976-1957 The Vac Shop
1956 J. Taylor
1955-1951 J. Tipping
1935-1930 F. Walshaw Fruiterer
1929-1913 W. Rylance Shopkeeper
1912 E. Beecroft Shopkeeper
1911-1906 Sarah A. Sellers

Disused inn, cottages and court rebuilt

Weavers Arms
Licence refused 1891
1891-1881 Michael Brannelly
1881-1860 Wm. Rourke
1859-1856 Geo. Kenworthy
1855-1854 Geo. Utley

New Street Inn
1868-1848 John and Charles Topham

Earlier map showing as far as Wood Street. Dotted lines indicate the Westway relief road.

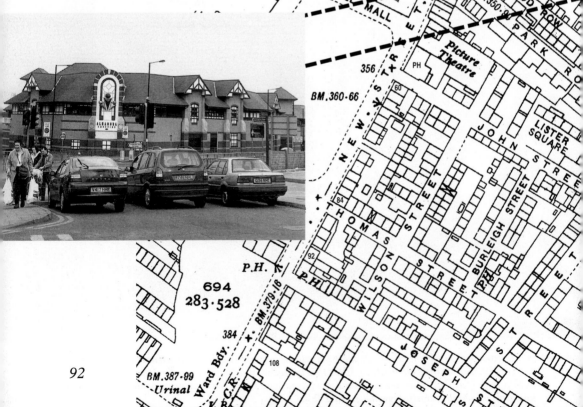

Numbers 28 to 30 in 1960.

Numbers 38 to 48, between Park Row and the Globe Cinema, in 1960.

─ 1990 Demolished ─

The Globe Cinema, built 1914, included three shops

54

1986-1982 Globe Theatre

1982-1960 Vacant

1960-1914 Globe Cinema (lattely a bingo hall)

58

1990 Vacant

1986 Alabama Alligator

Globe Inn

1978-1967 Stanley Parrott

1967-1954 Peter Light

1954-1951 Harry Bottomley

1951-1942 Wm. Hy. Godley

1942-1941 Clement Ramsden

1941-1936 Geo. Stacey

1936-1932 Joseph Wm. Raynor

1932 Ewart Sweetman

1932-1930 Walter Woodhouse

50

1985-1971 Mario Hairdressing

1970-1969 A. E. Chapman Co. Estate Agents

1968-1962 Vogue Hairdressing

1961-1959 H. H. Ellis Dressmaker

1958-1952 E. H. Fell Pet Shop

1951 E. Roberts

1951-1946 J. Mattocks Footwear

1945-1915 B.B.C.S. Wallpaper

52

1985-1974 Mario Hairdressing

1974-1969 Refuge Lending Society

1966 R. Stocks Son Estate Agents

1961-1960 Strand Libraries

1959 Delicatessen

1957-1951 E. H. Fell Pet Shop

1951-1948 J. Mattocks Footwear

1947 C. Marshall

1946 Albert Bennett

1937-1933 J. Bailey Sweets

1933-1923 T. F. Eason Sweets-Tobacco

1923-1920 M. Brandt

1920-1915 Walter Healey

G L O B E   E N T R A N C E

56

1986-1970 Jax Exchange Service

1969 S. Christopher Motoring School

1965-1962 Lodge and Hughes Overalls

1961 H. Taylor Toys

Pulled down

56

1920 Hy. Hinchcliffe

1915-1890 Tom Dennis Hairdresser

1889-1884 Joseph Beevors

1883 Wm. Crampton

1882 John Rhymer

1881 John Fox

Dog and Gun

1930-1925 Albert Winnard

1925-1923 James Plunkett

1923-1916 Mary A. Plunkett

1916-1912 Bartholomew Plunkett

1912-1894 Stephen Denton

58

1894-1883 Harry Sparks

1883-1877 John Savage

1877-1868 Charles Shirt

1867 Geo. Whitehead

1866-1864 Henry Guest

1863-1844 Wm. Goodworth Grocer

─ Rebuilt 1914 ─

50

1913-1908 R. Rusby Son Fishmonger

1905-1898 Charles V. Watts Glass and China

1897 C. Bird

1896 H. Hand

1895 Tom Brown

1894-1893 E. Fairbottom Fishmonger

1892 Geo. Bent

1891-1890 Joseph Beevors

1887-1881 Ann Cummings

52

1913-1911 G. Bradley Fried Fish

1910-1909 G. Thompson

1908-1906 Arthur Ramsden

1905-1903 C. Siddall Fried Fish

1903-1898 Mary A. Shaw Confectioner

1897 Ann Jenkins

1891-1890 Wm. Demaine

1889-1883 Ann Fairbottom

(George)

1882-1879 Tom Drury

1877-1871 Thomas Poppleton Fishmonger

87

1868-1833 Wm. King Cabinet Maker

54

1913-1906 J. Pointer

1905-1899 Wm. Fisher Confectioner

1898-1892 S. Beevors Grocer

(Joseph)

1891-1889 Ann Jenkins

1888-1887 Wm. Nixon

1885-1871 Geo. Bent

86

1870-1867 Hy. Wm. Howe

1866-1852 Joseph Poles Footwear

1851-1849 Ed Sullivan Tailor

1848 John Liveredge

Queen Victoria's Diamond Jubilee Medal.

When this picture was taken in the early 20th century straw hats were in fashion for men and women and voluminous pinafores were in vogue for small children.

When this inn was rebuilt the name was changed to conform with the adjacent Picture House. At that time picture going was popular and the cinema was a well known landmark.

This bingo hall (built as a bowling alley in the 1980s) and its car park now occupy the site of Rowland Winn Ltd, seen below in the 1960s.

John Street

60

2001-1999 Gala Bingo
1999-1996 Shipleys Bingo Hall
1996- c1983/4 Delta Bowling Alley

───── 1973-1967 Roland Winn Cars ─────   ───── 1973-1947 Roland Winn Cars ─────

60	62	64	66	68
1965-1960 Hawely Boot Repair	1965-1950 Sargeant Grocer	1947-1944 R. W. Squire	1936-1920 J. Wray Tripe	1936-1932 J. Coombes
1952-1944 R. W. Squire	1948-1937 Miss L. Gill	Bakehouse	Dresser	Footwear Repair
1941-1920 Kaye Smith Baker	1936-1922 W. Ogden	1941-1927 K. Smith	1915 E. Ward	1929 P. Greenwood
1915 Herbert Hinchcliffe	Shopkeeper	Bakehouse	1914 H. A. Dixon	Boot Shoe Dealer
1913 Harry Barnes	1921-1919 W. Edwards	1926-1907 W. Wright	1912-1910 J. Pointon	1922 A. Chappell Clogger
1912-1910 W. M. Grimwood	1918-1913 Mary Pointon	1906-1892 Arthur Sutcliffe	1909-1890 Henrietta Walker	1915-1914 A. Firth
Pledge Store	1912-1909 W. Kitching	Lamp Oil Dealer	1886 Wm. Walker	1913 M. E. Sutcliffe
1909-1906 Ely Blackwell	Shopkeeper	1891 R. Beecroft	1885 F. Kirk	1912 A. Firth
1905-1887 T. A. Atkinson Footwear	1908-1904 Wm. Thwaites	1889 Mary Hunt	1884 L. Cooke	1911-1910 J. Pointon
1886-1882 Wm. Berry	1903-1888 M. A. Braithwaite	1887 Wm. Hazelhurst	1883-1871 Geo. Wells	1909 T. H. Drinkwater
1881 R. Fisher	Grocer	1883-1868 Wm King	Shopkeeper	1908-1906 H. Newton
1877-1872 Kenny and Osbourne	1887 Wm. White			1905-1904 W. Austerfield
	1886 J. Atkinson			1903-1897 Jane Wood
	1885 J. Lockwood			1896 G. Barrett
	1880-1879 John Topham			1895-1889 Benj. Sutcliffe
	1878-1872 Hy. Mason			1887 Geo. Ennis
				1886-1884 E. Travis
				1883 J. Walker
				1881-1880 T. Frances
				1879-1878 F. Travis
				1877 H. Mason
				1876-1874 Richard Norris
				1873 J. Denton

83	82	81	80	79
1871 R. Gorrell	1871 R. Gorrell	1867-1861 John Bashforth	1870-1853 Caroline Roberts	1871 Robt. Halcock
1869 Geo. Beckett	1869 Thomas Rock	1860 Benj. Laycock		1870 John Barker
1868 Peter Duncan	1868 Peter Duncan	1859-1848 John Bashforth		1869-1860 Wm. Bedford
1867-1866 Charles Shirt	1867-1866 Charles Shirt	1847 Geo. Machin		1859-1854 Wm. Leech
1865-1848 Robt. Goodworth Grocer	1865-1848 Robt. Goodworth			
1847 Sarah Brook	Grocer			
	1847 Sarah Brook			

98

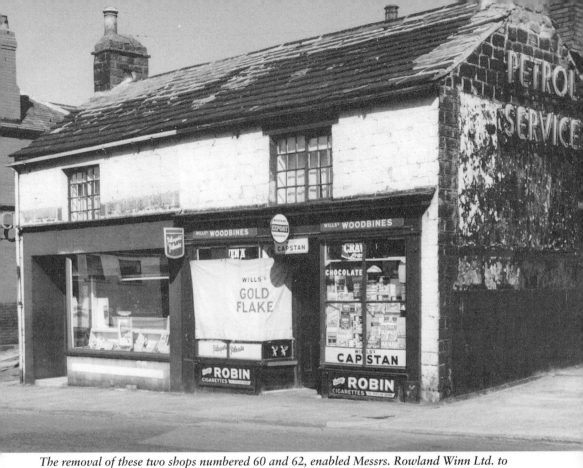

The removal of these two shops numbered 60 and 62, enabled Messrs. Rowland Winn Ltd. to enlarge their forecourt in the 1960s.

An example of how commercial property replaced a number of houses in this part of town. This is the corner of Thomas Street, in the 1960s. In 2001 both properties are still there.

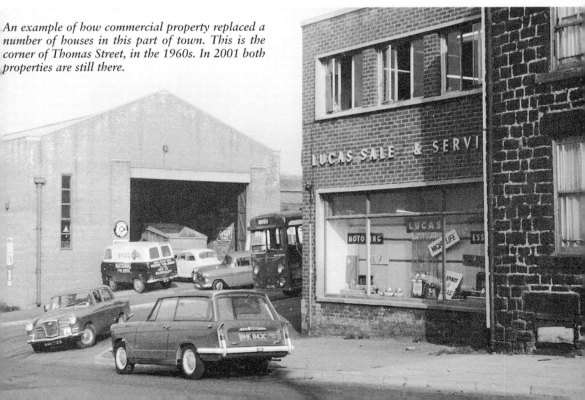

2001-2000 Empty
2000-1978? National Tyre
     and Auto Care
1978?-1971 Briggs Tyre Company
1970-1966 Yorkshire Tyre Co.

House Nos. 70-84 pulled
down 1958

No. 82/84

1930-1890 H. H. Cotterill Grocer
1888-1863 Benj. Rogers Grocer
1862-1851 James Rogers Grocer
1850-1844 Jane Parker

Thomas Street
In Thomas Street was the Earl of Stratford Inn

1911-1908 Joseph Gawthorpe	1871 William Wild
1908-1904 Richard Baker	1870-1869 William Dennis
1904-1898 Ann Freshney	1868-1866 Daniel Carnley
1898-1888 Jonathan Gill	1865 Charles Worrall
1888 Thomas Spurr	1864-1858 William Armin
1888-1887 Geo. Padgett	1857-1856 Richard Armin
1887-1886 Edmund Wike	1855 John Sykes
1886-1882 Joseph Grayson	1854-1849 Nancy Topham
1882-1881 Walter Dunk	1848-1837 Wm. Topham
1881-1872 John Dunk	

2001-1985 PARTCO
    Vehicle Parts
1985-? Lucas Car Electrical
197?-1951 Globe & Simpson

House Nos. 86-90 pulled
down 1936

92
1929-1905 E. Garbutt
    Furniture
    Broker
1904-1847 A. Firth

(George)

90

Demolished

94
1957-1956 L. Mann
1955 G. Wray

Commercial Inn
Closed Dec. 1953
1953-1945 Jane Shaw
1945-1937 Robert Shaw
1937-1931 James Moore
1931-1924 Geo. Allott
1924 Lily M. Dodd
1924-1913 Samuel Dodd
1913-1909 Wm. Simmon
1909-1900 Wm. Flowers
1900-1894 Harry Flower
1894-1881 Wm. Flowers

92
1881-1880 Thomas Turn
1880-1871 John Wilkins

65/66
1870-1866 John Hinchcl
1865-1864 John Wildsm
1863-1862 Sarah Hinch
1861-1854 Wm. Hinchcli
1852-1851 John Topham
1850-1849 Wm. Hinchcl
1848-1846 Geo. Wilkins
1845 John Digman
1844 John Parker
1842-1835 Michael Tierr
1830-1825 James Nixon

THE COMMERCIAL INN – which was licensed as early as 1825.

When this picture was taken the Commercial Inn had already lost its licence, and its front steps.
Houses behind the Commercial Inn were typical of houses in this area.

It is easy to see that here we have an example of what was originally a weavers cottage being converted into a shop. This frequently happened in New Street.

The appearance of this warehouse would suggest that it was formed from three houses. If that be so then the middle portion was the Cross Keys Inn. This building still stands in 2001 and can be seen in the smaller picture opposite.

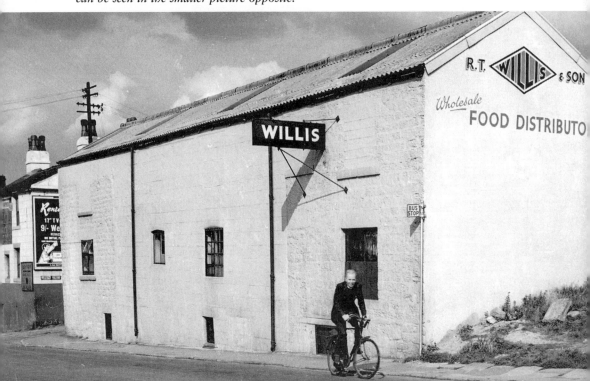

Joseph Street				Wood Street

Joseph Street

?-? Costcutter

1994-1952 R.T. Willis & Son
Wholesale Food
Distributor's

Houses Numbers 96 to 100
Pulled down or Converted
1935

Number 96 between 1868
and 1858 was the **Cross
Keys Inn**

Thomas Fairclough

Houses, Number 106
Pulled down 1959
Numbers 102 and 104
Pulled down 1935

108/110
1973 C. Lawson Newsagent
-1929 Geo. Gill Newsagent
1927-1885 H. Norton

(Fanny)

Demolished (date?)

Wood Street

In WOOD STREET were two inns

Woodman Inn
Closed 1929
1929-1925 William Jackson
1925-1924 Walter McDonald
1924-1916 Jane Parker
1916-1899 Elijah Parker
1899-1895 Albion Turner
1895 Mary A. Marsden
1895-1893 Charles Marsden

Wood Street Hotel
Closed 1966
1966-1965 Mildred Cross
1965-1964 Ronald Cross
1964-1955 Jack Fisher
1955-1949 John Dickinson
1949-1945 John Camplejohn
1945-1939 Colin Camplejohn
1939-1935 Percy Whittaker
1935-1928 Betsy Ann Whittaker
1928-1906 Wright Whittaker
1906-1893 Robert Cherry
1893 Joshua Leap
1893-1891 Thomas Bartholomew
1891-1890 Edwin Smart
1890-1889 Arcemus Buckley
1889-1888 William Lycett
1888-1884 Benj. Fairclough
1884-1872 Wm. Norman
1893-1891 Elizabeth Marsden
1891-1868 Wm. Marsden

Wood Street Hotel.

New Street

North Side

5

2001 - Empty
2001-1998 Just Right Clothes
1997-1968 Bailey's Baby Linen
1967-1958 Wakefield Army Stores
1957-1928 J. Hadwen Sons Outfitters
1927-1899 Geo. Owram Hosier
1898-1875 Alfred Crummack Hosier
1874-1865 John Aspinall Brush Maker

2

1864-1861 Geo. Owram
1860-1856 Wm. Bailey
1855-1851 John Hepworth Butcher
1850 Widow Horsfield
1849 Wm. Brocklebank
1847-1841 Geo. Owram
1840-1833 Mary Tyre
1825 James Sykes

3

2001-2000 Link Telecom
2000-1998 Handy Phones
1997-1978 Skinwear/Leatherwear
1977-1972 Suede & Leather Fashions/Skinwears
1971-1932 Cadmans Wallpaper
1931 D.C. Bailey
1930-1867 B. Owram Baby Linen

(Henry)

1

2001-1990 Snappies Photo processing
1990 Vacant
1990-1976 Farmers Butchers
1975-1952 Farm Stores (Farmers Butchers)
1961-1930 M. and G. Jackson Butchers

1928-1867 Geo. Owram Pork Butcher

(Henry)

1

Blue Bell Inn
License withdrawn 1866
John Hardcastle
1861 Joseph Hirst
1860-1849 Geo. Owram

Rebuilt 1849
1848-1825 Thomas Tyre

These two photographs of numbers 1, 3 and 5, show how properties can survive many years of change.

The lower part of New Street shown here was originally known as Newlands. It will be noticed that Mr. Gray is displaying a large pair of spectacles above his shop number 7, to indicate he is an optician.

A probable date of this photograph is 1910 which would account for the patriotic decorations for the Coronation of King George V.

13	**11**	**9A (upstairs)**	**9**	**7**
2001-1987 Help The Aged Charity Shop	2001-1982 Wordsworth Travel	2001 Empty	2001-1986 Staniforths Bakers	2001-2000 Direct Discounts Electrical Discount
1986 Vacant		2000-1994 Linda Elliott Associates Office Services	1986-1978 Mudds Bakers	2000-1995 Elegant Furnishers
1985 - Bodystone Health Studio			1978-1975 Empty	1995-1976 Bailey's Baby Linen
			1975-1969 Granada Television	1976-1956 Paragon Jewellers
			1968-1961 Robinsons Radio Rentals	1955-1945 J. Graham Furniture
			1960-1917 Fletcher & Frankland Hosiers	1944-1943 Franks Furniture
			1916 John Exley Draper	1940-1933 A. Hepworth Ladies Outfitter

13/11

1982-1978 Buyaround Offices
1977 Empty
1976-1975 Zodiac Carpets
1974-1973 Osbourne Organ Galleries
1970-1967 Wakefield Army Stores
1966-1962 Phillips Furnishing Store

(Elizabeth)

1932-1931 Green's Store Surplus Stock
1930-1929 Sheffield Wallpaper Co.
1927-1898 R.E. Gray Option
1897-1882 John Hirst
1881-1880 Wm. Senior Butcher

4

1860-1856 E. Abraham
1855-1841 Benny Hague Bookseller
1839 Geo. Bland Beerhouse
1835 S. Musgrave
1825 Thomas Robinson

3

(Samuel)
(William)
(Tailor)

———— Rebuilt 1961 ————

1960-1933 A. Schofield Confectioner	1960-1898 G. King and Son Fishmongers
1932-1922 G.F. Banks Tobacconist	1897-1860 Martha A. Fogg Fishmonger
1920-1906 W.L. Atkinson Tobacconist	
1905-1892 James Baron	(George)

5

18595-1854 Geo. Wike
1852-1844 John Hirst Carter
1842 I. Rhodes
1841 Wm. Wike
1839 Mrs. Fox

Numbers 5, 3 and 1 in the 1960s.

Here New Street and Cheapside join forming a continuous frontage, before the numbering of shops this led to some confusion in this area. Above, probably 1955 as J. Graham was closing, and below in 1960.

21

2001 Big Apple Schoolwear
2001-1994 Rubens Menswear
1994-1990 Vacations Travel
1990-1988 Cockcroft Travel Agent
1987-1982 Ashley Adams
     Travel Agent
1978 Vacant
1977-1974 New Street Furnishers
1974-1971 Empty
1971-1934 Millers Bargain Store
1932-1901 G. Gordon Costumier

(Gordon and Dutch)

1902-1898 Billington Lung Balsam Co.
1897 J.L.P. Hollingworth Chemist
1891-1888 F. Billington
1887-1884 Wm. White
1883-1879 Thomas J. White
1878 Thomas Reed
1877 James Jackson

9

1876-1861 Geo. Hayes Pork Butcher
1859-1844 Thomas Goodaire Butcher

19

1976 Demolished to widen
    Hayes Croft
1969-1899 W. Blackburn Co.
    Outfitters
1897-1894 Grant and Co
1893-1891 Hy. W. Howe
1890 Henry Thresh
1887-1868 James Wood
1867-1862 Scales and Salter
1859-1850 John McDoul
    Shoemaker
1849-1847 John Smith
1846-1841 Ann Hughes

Hayes Croft

17/15

2001-1980 Pinocchio's Restaurant

17

1979-1970 Vacant
1970-1940 J. Lodge & Son
    Newsagents
1938-1932 A. Pritchard Fruiterer
1932-1929 Lawson & Eagle
1928-1912 M. J. Fletcher Draper
1911-1910 Mary E. Hyslop
1909-1897 S. W. Webster Tobacconist
1896-1894 Wm. Wood
1893-1872 Hy. W. Howe

7

1870 John Thresh
1868-1860 Dominic Clary
1859 M. Donoghue
1875-1835 Peter Carney Lodging House
1833-1830 Richard Clarke
1825 John Turner

15

1979-1970 Vacant
1970-1949 Brighter Homes Wallpaper
1948-1938 Farm Stores Ltd.
1938 C. Guymer
1937 Walter Brown
1936-1928 F. Smales Butcher
1927-1926 Barnard Bankrupt Stock
1925-1894 I. Pryor Jeweller
1893-1871 John Charlesworth

6

1870 John Thresh
1868-1864 Wm. Fieldhouse Footwear
1845 John Dale
1844 Richard Thorpe
1842-1830 Richard Goodair Butcher
1825 Jeremiah Gillott

A view of the lower part of New Street about 1900. Facing up the street is John Charlesworth's shop in Sheffield Road.

Here we see number 7 in the 1880s when Mr. Senior was in occupation.

Number 7 can still be seen to the right of this picture in 2001.

HAYES CROFT

Hayes Croft was occupied by a number of small businesses and workshops. This was mostly swept away in the 1970s and 1980s, first by the development of the Tesco Store in Albert Street East, and then by the subsequent enlargement of Boots store (taking over the Tesco premises) and new shops in Albert Street East.

We do not have detailed records of businesses in Hayes Croft, but with the assistance of former occupants have been able to provide this 'snapshot' of the thriving community working there in the 1960s and 1970s. To avoid confusion identifying the properties, we have lettered them, as shown on the plan.

19 New Street: demolished in 1971 to widen Hayes Croft. The rear of 21 New Street was then occupied by Bainbridge and Gibbons, dentists. Mr Gibbons is still there.

A: At one time used by George Owram as slaughter house for his butchers shop at 1 New Street. In the 1950s, J.R. Steel DIY. From c1960 - c1987, Woodworkers Supplies, run by Roland Owram. (G. Owram was the uncle of R. Owram and owned this and properties B-G. After his death the properties were managed by Trustees of his estate).

B: Jim Croft, signwriter, there 1950s to c1961.

C: Wilf Whysall, plumber, 1959 to 1979.

D: Used as a store by Woodworkers Supplies (A).

E: Frank Sawyer, locksmith until 1970s, then rented by D. Porteous (F) until demolished in c1982.

F: Before 1946 was a bakehouse. 1946 to 1986, D. Porteous and Son, upholsterers. Upper floor was rented to french polishers; first Ernest Pool, mid/late 1960s, then Don Hebden, c1972 to 1986.

G: Oldfields Bakery until c1970. Peter Tomlinson, joiner, until c1978, then Don Hebden, french polisher, until 1986.

H: Albert Hirst, pork butcher and processor, until 1970s.

J. Jack Richardson, shoe repairer.

K. Used as rear premises of Co-op store in Cheapside.

For those properties shown on the plan as numbered in Albert Street East, we have some information.

10: Howes tripe preparation (the tripe was delivered by motorcycle and sidecar).
12-14: Gill, wholesale Sunday newsagent, later moved to Doncaster Road.

110

1960s views of Hayes Croft from New Street (left) and from Albert Street East (right).

When the shutters were removed frm Mr. King's shop, number 11, there was exposed an open fishmongers slab. This shop and Schofields were demolished and rebuilt in 1961.

The corner shop occupied by J. Lodge and Son was the third shop on this side of New Street which they had occupied. To the left is Hayes Croft.

27

2001-1993 Grove Home Textiles
1993-1988 Hi Tan Solarium
1986 Vacant
1985-1975 Motorists Discount Store
1975-1970 B.B.C.S Nursery
1970-1943 B.B.C.S. Wallpaper Dept.
1939-1895 J. Lodge Son Newsagents
1894-1886 Alfred Whitham Printer
Post Office

1885-1880 A. Whitham	1885-1883 L. Cassigranda
1877-1873 Edwin Gelder	1881 J. Ibberson
1871 Martha Ash	1878 T. Rathray
1870 Geo. Woodruff	1877-1870 Edwin Gelder
1869-1862 John Thresh	Footwear
1860-1854 Joseph Beck	
1852-1849 Widow Melody	**12**
1848-1846 Joseph Gibbons	1869 Arthur Woodruff
1845-1841 Richard Ellison	1867-1860 Benj. Wright
1839 Wm. Parr	1859-1844 Thomas Coward
	Tailor
	1843-1842 Thomas Wilson
	1841 Thomas Coward
	1839 I. Sedgwick

25

2001 Rubens Mens, Youths, Boys Wear
2001-1985 Big Apple Clothing Leatherwear
1985-1979 Brian Barnard Furit/Veg
1978 Vacant
1977-1950 Dewhurst Butchers
1949-1911 W. R. Fletchers Ltd. Butchers
1909-1906 A. Bowring
1905-1869 Harry Bailey Pork Butcher

(George)

11

1868-1867 James Smeaton
1866-1844 Geo. Hoyland Footwear
1842-1841 Sammuel Birks

23

2001-1986 Arnolds Jewellers
1986 Vacant
1985-1982 Print Box, Art Materials
1978-1976 Walker Cheeseman Office Stationers
1976-1971 Empty
1971-1958 G. A. Woodcock Travel Agent
1958-1949 Norah Gowns
1948 Ibberson Gowns
1939-1935 Grimsby Trawler Fisheries
1934-1931 L. Rusby
1927-1912 W. Frudd Hairdresser
1911 Empire Record Co.
1910 Clara Miller
1909 Geo. Brettener

(Uriah)

1874-1869 Charles Ledger Hairdresser

10

1868 Uriah Brettoner
1867 Francis Colley
1866-1865 John Aspinall
1864-1863 Andrew Wilson
1861-1850 Geo. Hayes Pork Butcher
1894-1844 Peter Hoey
1843 Wm. Lewis
1841 John Bray

Numbers 15 and 17, seen opposite, has been Pinocchio's restuarant for over twenty years.

At the rear of these shops, 19 and 21 was a gymnasium and here also was the meeting of Toc H.

31/29

2001-1985 P & J Textiles Home Sewing Centre
1985 Vacant
1985-1974 Contractors Sales
1973 Empty
1972-1969 B.B.C.S. Toys
1968-1921 B.B.C.S. Radios and Television

31	29
1920-1912 Clara Miller Milliner	1919-1866 Mrs F. Bent
Friendship Inn	Butcher
1910-1894 Wm. Mills	(Aaron)
1894-1893 Joseph Coates	
1893-1880 Elijah Waller	1865 Thomas Clay
1879-1871 Patrick Ferrigan	1862-1849 Joseph
1870 Hy. Hodgson	Thornton
1869 James Garretty	1862-1849 Joseph
1868-1864 Pat Skelley	Broadhead
1863 G. H. Heap	Druggist
1862 Geo. Kitching	
1861-1860 Aaron Bent	
1859-1852 Henry Place	
1852-1851 John Wilson	
1847 Thomas Dailey	

Between 1859 and 1847 the house may not have been licensed.

Numbers 23, 25 and 27 in 1960. At the end of 19th century the shop next to the letter box was a Post Office. Here was printed Whitlam's Almanack which with Lodges Almanack contain much local information. Above, the same view in 2001.

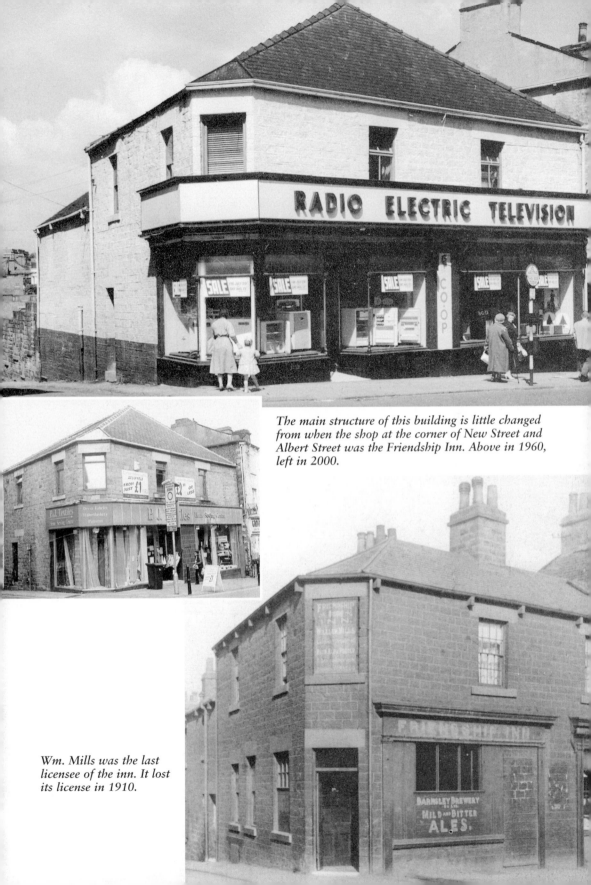

RADIO ELECTRIC TELEVISION

The main structure of this building is little changed from when the shop at the corner of New Street and Albert Street was the Friendship Inn. Above in 1960, left in 2000.

Wm. Mills was the last licensee of the inn. It lost its license in 1910.

The view from 'Island Corner' in 1893/4, when Joseph Coates ran the Friendship Inn.

33

2001-1999 Sense Charity Shop
1990-1978 B.B.C.S. Carpets
1975-1963 B.B.C.S. Grocery Dept.

Trafalgar Hotel

Closed April 1961, rebuilt

1961-1960 John C. Hayes	1954-1934 John White
1960-1958 Martin F. Hogad	1934-1933 John Ward
1958-1957 Patrick J. Burke	1933-1932 Geo. Stenton
1957 James P. Burke	1932-1930 John Hirst
1957-1956 Jack Mitchell	1930-1924 William Ramskill
1956-1955 Henry Taherny	1924-1922 Ronald Parkins
1955-1954 Patrick J. Burke	1922-1917 Harry P. Lewis

1917-1914 Alice Parkins
1914-1905 James Parkins
1905-1897 Joseph Hart
1897-1871 Charles Shaw
1870-1869 John Brown

1868-1855 Geo. Bailey Grocer	Trafalgar Hotel
	1868-1867 John Brown
1854-1851 Geo. Sykes	1866-1862 Ed. Bradley
1850 John Lodge	1861-1841 Joseph Sykes

Albert Street

In Albert Street was the
O'Connel Arms
1868-1866 Ed. Devine

White Lion
1865-1859 Geo. Winter

The hotel was built by Joseph Sykes who was the first landlord and it remained an hotel for 120 years. The adjoining shop became part of the hotel in 1869.

In the early 1960s the Trafalgar Hotel was replaced by a new Co-op grocery store, below. Above, the same building in 2001.

2001-1994 Club Hedonism and Hedon Rock Cafe Bar
1994 Vacant
1990-1903 B.B.C.S. Drapery Dept.

45

1902 C. Burnett Fried Fish
1897-1896 R. Griffiths
1895 G. Neil
1894 L. Newton
1893-1892 Wm. Hirst
1891-1887 Thomas Padgett
1886 Wm. Beldam
1874-1870 Thomas Cooper Greengrocer

23

1869-1857 Wm. Hayes Greengrocer
1856-1849 Samuel Fieldsend Cord Wainer
1848-1844 Samuel Saul
1842-1837 Geo. Peckett Shopkeeper

43

1902-1895 John C. Wormald Confectioner
1894 F. Wright
1893-1886 M. Haywood
1884 S. Ward
1883-1881 Bernard Wogan
1880-1875 Hy. Curtis
1874-1873 Ed. Brisby

22

1872-1857 James Walton
1856-1837 Mary Sykes
Supported by a mangle

41

1902-1896 Mrs Farmer Shopkeeper
1895-1891 Sarah Hopes
1889 James Holmes
1887 C. Walshaw
1886 Emily Curtis
1885-1883 James Denton
1882-1872 Joseph Hardcastle

21

1871 Harriet Horsley
1870-1868 Anthony Edson
1866 Mary Beachill
1865 James Wilkinson
1864-1856 Peter Atkinson
1855-1854 Thomas Dennis
1853-1850 Richard Bowling
1849 John Greenwood
1848-1837 John Senior Butcher

(George)

39

1902-1883 Caroline Wilson
Confectioner
1881-1879 Wm. Crompton
1878 E. Riddiough
1876-1845 Wm. Broadhead
Shoemaker

20

1844 John Trafford

The crowd gathered outside the Friendship Inn was probably waiting for the latest news for this is one of the places where in the nineteenth century the latest national and regional information was given. On the left is the first shop opened by Jabez Lodge in 1871.

'Island Corner'   Wellington Street

2001-1994 Club Hedonism and Hedon Rock Cafe Bar
1994 Vacant
1990-1886 B.B.C.S. Drapery Dept.
1885-1880 B.B.C.S. Warehouse
1873-1805 New Connexion Methodist Chapel

37

1902-1900 B.B.C.S. Fish Dept.
1899-1876 Jabez Lodge Newsagent
1875-1872 Ellen Kaye

19

1871 Elijah Broadhead
1870-1854 Frances Lodge
(John)

1852-1850 Wm. Ball
1849 Hy. Carr
1848 Thomas Jessop
1847-1845 Thomas Gardner
1844 Wm. Yates

35

1902-1900 B.B.C.S. Fish Dept.
1899-1871 Jabez Lodge Newsagent

18

1870-1869 Wm. Cartwright Shopkeeper
1868-1867 John Nichols
1866-1862 Chas Woodruff Prams etc.
1861-1860 John Nichols
1859-1857 Reynolds
1856-1852 Rev. C. Hibbert
1851 Rev. Wm. Innocent
1850 Rev. Laxton
1848 Rev. J. Curtis
1847 Rev J. Nelson
1845 Rev. Seaton
1844 Thomas Farrow

Interior of the B.B.C.S. Tinning Dept.

This property was bult at different times. The lower portion, on the right was built in 1886 and the upper portion in which iron work was used in 1903.

49/47

c1986 Demolished for new road

Empty 1972

49

1970-1969 White Rose School
of Motoring

47

1971 B.B.C.S. Optical Dept

1970 Hibbert, Ashton and
Youel Stationers

1968 White Rose school
of Motoring

1967-1910 B.B.C.S. Hardware Dept.

1905-1903 John C. Wormald Confectioner	1902-1898 Patrick McCoy Grocer
1902-1897 Fred Potter Draper	1897 W. Oates
1896-1894 Jesse Hepworth	1896 Frances Braithwaite
1891-1890 John Lee	1881-1866 Wm. Gainster Grocer
1887-1886 Fred Potter	
1885-1883 T. Mould	
1880-1877 John Rhymer	**24**
1876-1869 Wm. B. Beldam Grocer	1865-1855 John Charlesworth
	1854-1825 Frances Bennett Grocer

25

1868-1856 John Wells

1855-1844 Peter Atkinson Shuttlemaker

1842-1825 Wm. Hoadley

This picture of the shop is a frame from a cinema advertisement used locally.

Numbers 47 and 49 in 1960. Behind was an extensive warehouse in later years used for storage but earlier it was where Tinning was carried on.

Sailor Boy Inn

Closed January 1932

1932-1931 Joseph W. Raynor
1931-1930 James Moore
1930-1929 Geo. Wm. Cooper
1929-1924 Joseph Gawthorpe
1924-1922 Clara Exley
1922-1911 Joseph Shirt
1911-1909 Larriat Naylor
1909-1906 Alfred Atha
1906-1899 Barnabas Gill
1899-1890 Thomas Stanley
1890-1886 John Mullaney
1886- Geo. Hardy
1886-1882 Wm. Shaw
1882 Peter Hoey
1882-1881 Robt Whitham
1881-1879 John Mullaney
1879-1878 Frances E. Craven
1878-1874 Thomas Latham
1874-1862 Charles Simmons
1861-1854 James Smith
1852 Wm. Ross
1851-1848 Geo. Utley
1847-1841 Thomas Acklam

Houses 87-79 Pulled down 1929	**THOMAS STREET**	Houses 77-75 Pulled down 1929	**HAWKSWORTH SQUARE**	Houses 73-51 Pulled down 1929	**PALL MALL**

IN PALL MALL

In PALL MALL were two beerhouses which existed for only a short time.

Hope and Anchor Inn
1868-1859 William Roobottom

Horse and Jockey Inn
1868-1860 George Fearn
1859 Lydia McMahon

A picture of the Sailor Boy Inn when Alfred Atha was landlord between 1909 and 1906. The little Alice in Wonderland wearing laced boots appears a lonely figure.

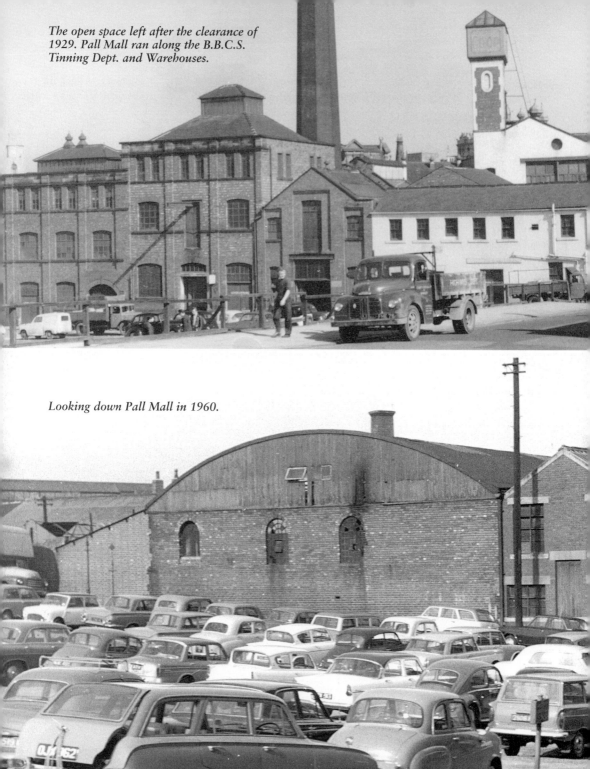

The open space left after the clearance of 1929. Pall Mall ran along the B.B.C.S. Tinning Dept. and Warehouses.

Looking down Pall Mall in 1960.

Above. In 2001. The new road crosses in front of the white Co-op building, now Club Hedonism.

WELLINGTON STREET
EAST SIDE

NB. Corner Pin (included with Peel Sq) is actually no 2 Wellington St.

4

2001-1968 Ted Hairdresser
1967-1958 T. Simpson Hairdresser
1957-1922 E. Longbottom Hairdresser
1914 Alf Thorpe
1912 Benj. Goodliffe
1910 Wm. Stanley
1909 M.A. Powell
1906-1905 T. Morgan Fried Fish
1902-1895 Lily Hey Fried Fish
1894 M. Overton
1883 John Brook

6/8

2001-1999 Wellington Street Chippie
1999-1986 Mike Lee Travel

6

1982-1947 E. Banks Confectioner
1936-1933 A. Corker Furniture Broker
1927 C. Thresh Newsagent
1909-1897 A. Wainwright Confectioner
1896-1895 S. Brocklebank
1894-1890 J. Harrison
1888-1884 Wm. J. Chappell
1883 T. Wright
1882 Charles Hodges
1880-1879 Leonard Land
1878-1875 Ann Hey
1874-1872 Edward Cooke

27

1870-1855 John Stringer

8

1982-1932 E. Banks Confectioner
1932 W. W. Crabtree Electrical Engineer
1910-1880 E. Wainwright Furniture
1879-1845 Mary Goodyear Milliner

26

No.8 upstairs

2001 Vacant
2000-1991 The Room Hair Design
(Moved to 9-11 Pitt St)

Entranc **to** **Car Par**

The side of the Corner Pin Inn and numbers 4, 6 and 8. Between 1909 and 1899 in the Corner Pin Yard was J.R. Thresh, paper merchant who succeeded J.H. Thackson. Seen here in 1960, opposite in 2001.

Wellington Street c1960. The lines indicate the relief road and roundabout.

Reproduced from the Ordnance Survey map with the permission of Ordnance Survey on behalf of Her Majesty's Stationery Office, © Crown Copyright MC 100035068

10/12/14/16

2001-1998 The Sport 2 Bar Licencee Darrell Mitchell

1998-1986 M & V Kitchen Centre

1983-1965 Lowrance Reynolds and Wadsworth Ironmongers

1965-c1954 Eric Banks Ltd

Archway | 18

10	**12**	**14**	**16**	
House	1941-1933 T. Tomlinson Accountant	1953 W.M. Langdale Overalls	1951-1936 S. Eaton Hairdresser	
	1930 R.C. Hoyle	1936 G. Hill Cycle Agent	1933-1919 G. Lunn Fruiter	
	1929-1913 F.I. Bedford Engraver	1929 W. Swift	1915-1906 M. Lee Fruiterer	
	1912 A. Slack Herbalist	1922 J. Hutchinson Dentist	1905 A. Gill Fruiterer	
	1910-1906 D. C. Bridge	1920 E. Dobson		
	1905 J. Raynor Stationer	1918 J. Boothroyd		
		1915-1912 Wm. Turner		
		1910-1906 T.G. McLoughlin Hairdresser		
		1905 W. Kaye Tobacconist		

18

2001-1998 Incorporated into Sport 2 Bar

1998-1983 J. Hartley Ltd. Ironmo

1983-1980 J & J. Hartley Dawn Rose Babywea

1978-1972 Geo. Horsewood Betting Shop

1971-1952 Harry Ennis Betting Shop

1939-1923 G. A. Habbershon Confectioner

1922-1912 Mrs A. Hunt Shopkeeper

1910-1906 Janet Dale Sweets. Biscuits

1905 Susan Blackburn

—————————— New Property ——————————

1896-1871 Barnsley Corporation Waterworks Dept.

1868-1865 James Simmons

1864-1862 Geo. Birkinshaw

1860-1845 Matthias Wood Plumber

In 1965 numbers 10 to 16 were converted by Messrs Lowrance, Reynolds and Wadsworth into one shop. Two old established firms of iron mongers who had traded separately came together. Both started trading on Market Hill. Reynolds and Wadsworth opened in 1871 and Joseph Lowrance was there in 1820.

20

2001-1996 Blackburns Cafe

1996-1982 Russel Eaton Ladies Hair Stylist

1978-1977 Leather Fayre

1976-1975 Closed

1974-1962 Dolland & Aitcheson Optician

22

2001-1996 Lagoon Hair Design

1996-1982 Russell Eaton Gents' Hair Stylist

1982-1962 Bretton School of Motoring

24

2001-1997 Franklin Pizza Delivery

1996-1968 The Lighting Centre

1968-1962 South Yorkshire Motor Insurance Co.

24A (upstairs)

2001-1994 Personnel Evaluation Consultants

1994-1991 S.J.J. Consultants

?-1962 Co-operative Insurance Society

—————————— Rebuilt 1960 ——————————

20

1960-1872 J.J. Park Watchmaker

1871 Thomas Foster

1870-1859 Benj. Hague

1857-1854 Charles Osbourne

22

1960 J.V. Grimes Battery Dept.

1936 Mrs. H. Marshall

1929-1923 A. Hepworth Draper

1922 D. Cohen Smallware

1920-1907 Mrs. Taylor (Edward)

1906-1904 Tom Morgan

1902-1899 Lily Hey

1898-1890 Wm. Hirst

1888-1887 Mrs. Hey

1886-1878 Joseph Hammerton

1877-1876 J.A. Crawshaw

1874-1873 John B. Fletcher

1871-1863 Wm. Allas

1862-1855 John Cooke

Archway

1938-1923 N. Lumb Son Rag Dealer

1922 A. Rawson

1906-1901 Geo. Thompson

1896-1894 James Coates

1893 Wm. Overton

1892-1886 Eli Prewer

24

1960 Fells Pet Shop

1949-1937 E. Senior Engraver

1936 Mrs. H. Marshall Newsagent

1929-1902 Mrs. T. Batty Confectioner

1901-1884 Samuel Gill

1883-1881 Wm. Sheers

1880-1873 Wm. Hy. Horne

1871-1856 Saul Neatby

1855-1846 Hy. Clegg

(John)

These modern shops replaced earlier shops, numbers 20 to 24, in 1960.

Mr. John James Park opened this shop, number 20 in 1872 and it was not closed until 1960.

The Barnsley British Cooperative Society Library. In the original volume this was described as built in 1935. However the frontage bears the carved words, 'Central Chambers 1914'. To the left are numbers 20-24 before the 1960 rebuilding.

26	28/30	32
2001-1991 What Everyone Wants rear of	2001-1896 Salvation Army Citadel	2001- Bar '1' Licencee Brett Thompson
1990 Co-op Store		1990-1986 The Video House
1986-1976 B.B.C.S. Prams		1978-1940 B.B.C.S.
Closed July 1971		1940-1935 Barnsley Council of Social Services
1971-1935 B.B.C.S. Library		1933-1899 Barnsley District Grocers

1912-1896 Ed Cooke	1922 Central W.M. Club	1922-1907 Cooperative Employees Institute
	1905-1902 John Woodruff Boot Maker	1908-1907 Silver Band
	1901-1895 T. R. Waterton	1905-1899 Socialists Club
	1894 Hy. Burrows	

1893-1891 J. Longbottom Foundry and Yard
1886-1868 Wm. Neatby and Son Saw Mill
1866 Joseph Shaw Foundry and Wood Yard

The Salvation Army Citadel was built in 1896.

The Adult School 1971-1897 is the central building. It and the buildings on the right were demolished in 1971 to form the present car park.

Barnsley British Cooperative Society Offices.

34		**36**		2001-1998 Wellington House Barnsley Council Building	
2001-1973 Car Park				1990 B.B.C.S. Offices	1990 B.B.C.S. Supermarket
		———— Pulled Down 1971 ————		1973-1938 B.B.C.S. Offices	1973-1873 B.B.C.S. Shops
1971-1897 Adult School		Warehouse			
		1902-1899 Wm. Bramby Confectioner	1905-1902 A. Hawley Saw Mill	1937-1893 Houses 36 to 58	1912-1890 Armitage Co. Rag Merchant

The BBCS shops in 1960 (below) and as Barnsley Council offices in 2001 (right).

Barnsley British Cooperative Society shops.

The grocery department at the top of Market Street, into which the Cooperative Society moved after a few months trading in their first rented shop. They were demolished (below) and re-built in 1911, as seen opposite.

The Barnsley British Cooperative Society shops seen from New Street in 1960. The ground floor frontages were later crudely modernised, as can be seen in the 2001 view above.

WELLINGTON

WEST SIDE

7/5

2001-1996 The Ticket Office and Mustangs Bars
(Part of Wellington St. complex Licencee John Brookes)

3/1

2001-1998 The Hot House Takeaway

Chennels Bar

2001-2000 C. Bristowe
2000-1978 P. Bristowe
1978-1976 T. North
1976-1967 Ronald T. Yarker
1967-1966 Victor E. Crocker

———— 1990-1986 Home Electrical Discount Centres ————

1966-1964 John Mitchell
1964-1962 Jack Brook

7

1982-1949 P. Dante Tailor
1936 Fabrica Dyers-Cleaners
1929-1920 J. Brundenell Dentist
1915 Saul Cresswell
1915-1901 A. H. Holder Chemist

5

1982-1976 Needle Craftts Haberdashery
1975-1972 Tony Briggs Fishing Tackle
1960 D-EM Bielby Fishing Tackle
1936 M. Grant Hairdesser
1930 M. Hirst
1927-1912 G. H. Frudd Confectioner
1910-1907 Ely Barker
1906-1901 Elizabeth Gillatt Confectioner

1976-1972 Mervyn Forbes Business Equipment
1971-1934 Yorkshire Evening Post

1927 AE-GH Townend
Draper
1915-1914 A. Wainwright
1913 Wm. Wilkinson
1911-1910 W. Brook
Confectioner
1909-1906 Albert Mitchell
1905-1900 Mrs. Clayton
Confectioner

1934-1933 A. Senior Son
Tailor
1930-1900 J. Coates
Accountant

1962 Arthur D. Francis
1962-1961 Norman P. Donnelly
1961-1958 Bernard D. Coyle
1958-1956 Clifford G. Amos
1956-1946 Bernard J. Hale
1946-1931 John S. Nottage
1931-1924 Percy A. Armstrong
1924-1919 Matthew Armstrong
1919-1897 James G. Chennell
and Wm. A. Armstron
1897-1876 Geo. Horne
1876-1835 Wm. J. Dandison

Chennel's Bars in 1960 (above) and 2001 (below).

These shops numbered 1 to 7 were built in 1990 on the site of two dwellings and Theatre Yard in which were seven cottages.

Theatre Royal

2001-1996 The Theatre Bar part of Wellington St. complex licencee John Brookes

1996-1990 Empty

1990-? Theatre Royal Bingo

?-1816 Theatre Royal

1898 Theatre enlarged

1884 Used as Salvation Army Barracks

1878 Used as Hall of Mechanics Institute

When this photograph was taken in 1960 the Theatre Royal, on the right, was a Bingo Hall. Morton's Cafe is now the Soviet Bar, seen above in 2001. It had been a fried fish shop for 102 years.

Castlereagh Street

Vacant Site
Houses
Numbers 15-17
Pulled down
1938

Shakespeare Hotel

1996-1982	R. Caddick
1982-1964	Donald Wm. Senior
1964-1952	Maurice Tate
1952-1945	Arthur Richardson
1945-1940	Joseph Sharpe
1940-1937	Percy Whittaker
1937-1924	Mary N. Booker
1924-1899	Geo. A. Dearden
1899-1895	Wm. Chatterton
1895-1891	Marcia Brook
1891-1890	John Brook
1890-1889	Charles E. Ullathorne
1889-1884	Wm. Bonson
1884-1871	John Taylor
1870-1867	John Rose
1866-1865	Hy. Blackwell
1864	John Bennett
1863	Hannah Sedgwick
1862	John May
1861	Edward Smith
1860	Hy. Hinchcliffe
1859-1858	Benj. Harrison
1857	Wm. Spink
1856	Geo. Buckley
1855-1854	Geo. Bonson
1852-1851	Mrs. Wilcock
1850-1846	Henry Wilcock
1845-1841	Geo. Broadhead
1839	Joseph Miller
1837-1822	Geo. Miller

1883-1880 Geo. Jackson
1877-1871 John Schofield
Top Boot Maker
1870 James Youell
1861-1860 S. Neatby Book
Binder
1859-1851 Ed Daniels
1847-1845 Thomas Walker
1844 Saul Merryweather
1843-1830 Joseph Woodiwis

11

1996-1966	Madge's Cafe
1967-1958	Betty's Cafe
1939-1938	P. Whittaker
1937	H. N. Booker
1936-1908	J.R. Steele
	Tripe Dresser
1907-1906	J. Langhton
1905	Geo. Jackson Tripe Dresser
1883-1866	Geo. Jackson
1865-1855	John Coke
	(Barnsley Flour Corn Co.)
1851-1841	John Stringer
1839-1835	Thomas Marshall
1833	John Midgley
1830	Joseph Whitehead

9

2001 Opened March 2000
The Soviet Bar part of
Wellington St. complex
1999-1995 Empire Fisheries
1994-1939 Morton's Fish Bar
1939-1923 J. A. Hopes Fried
1922-1918 M. Franks Fried F
1914-1904 M. Lee Fried Fish
1903-1897 G. H. Buckley Frie
1896-1890 John Jennings
1885-1878 Edward Cooke
1877-1871 Benj. Fearne
Glass China Dir.

Malt Shovel Inn

1868-1865 Wm. Collumbine
1864-1859 John Rimmington

Omar Pasha Inn

1857-1856 Benj. Harrison
1855 Richard Rogers
1854 Richard Carr
1853 Geo. Drake
1852 Daniel Padgett
1851 Mary Beaumont
1850-1837 Geo. Beaumont
1835-1825 Widow Batty

The Shakespeare and the Soviet Bar in 2001.

Shakespeare Hotel. This was the first hotel to be opened in the street.

Castlereagh Street. In the distance can be seen the spire of Holy Road Church. Left in 1960; above, in 2001 with the street now cut off by the relief road.

25	23	21	21/Upstairs	19
2001-1992 Tut and Shive	1990 Atlas Insurance	2001-1982 Croppers Hair Salon	2001-1998 Devil Bitch Tattoo Studio Pro Body Piercing	2001-2000 Cha Chaz Takeaway Food
1992-1986 Silvers Public House	1986-1969 Chapman & Co. Estate Agents	1982 Vacant		1998-1986 Globe Coaches
1982 Rose and Thistle	1966 J. Hoyle	1982-1961 Alan Clough Haberdashery		1986-1961 Kard Korner
Rose and Thistle Inn		1960-1837 House		1960-1954 G. I. Fretwell
?-1959 Rowland Midgley				1953-1918 E. C. Larcombe Shopkeeper
1959-1955 John L. Wallace				1914-1896 Wm. Stanley Grocer
1955-1951 Robt. Poskitt				1895-1861 Richard Royston Shopkeeper
1951-1941 Laura Haigh				1860-1859 Thomas Darby
1941-1930 Harry Haigh				1857 Geo. Gill
1930-1925 Charles Wm. Bird				1856-1851 John Bygate Boot Maker
1925-1923 Joseph S. Kershaw				1850-1849 John Gomersall
1923-1922 Allen Porter				1848 Hy. Hyde
1922-1915 Alfred Porter				1847 Wm. Hoyland Butcher
1915-1897 Herbert Porter				1846 Saml. Thornton
1897-1866 Geo. Barstow				1845-1844 Benj. Hinchcliffe
1865-1858 Henry Coles				1842-1837 Robt. Harrison
1857-1839 James Clarkson				

Shop at the corner of Wellington Street and Castlereagh Street, in the 1960s and (opposite) in 2001.

Above: Rose and Thistle Inn, now somewhat altered (below right) as The Tut and Shive.

29

2001-2000 Pulse Bar
        Licencee A. Asgari

-1990 Peels Cafe Bar

1986 Ring O'Bells

Ring O' Bells

1972-1970 Thomas Beevers

1970-1966 Ronald Cross

1966-1964 Jack Davies

1964-1939 Afred Robinson

1939-1934 Thomas Birkett

1934-1930 Alice Gaut

1930-1917 Wm Gaut

1917-1907 Alfred Giggall

1907-1899 John Wm. Sizer

1899-1895 Catherine McMamion

1895-1893 John McMamion

1893-1890 John Roach

1890-1882 John Brook

1882-1878 John Swift

1878-1876 Samuel Beachill

1876-1871 Mary Ibberson

1870-1869 Wm. Ibberson

1868-1866 Mary Mallinson

1865-1858 Wm. Mallinson

1857-1855 Thomas Firth

Vacant Site

Houses Numbers 25-27
Pulled down 1937

Foundry Street

2001-1998 Pharaoh's Night Club
        Licencee Kevin Proctor

1997-1960 Radical and Liberal Club

Vacant Site

1912-1906 T. Kenworthy Co. Foundry

1905-1882 Kenworthy Taylor Co. Foundry

1881-1875 Kenworthy and Atkinson Foundry

1874-1848 John Shaw Foundry and Dye Works

1847-1836 Young and Shaw Foundry

1835-1825 Young and Athorn

Wortley Street

Pharoah's Night Club.

Francis Jordan House in the centre of this picture replaced the shops seen opposite.

Foundry Street is so called because of the foundry which was in this area until 1912. This photograph was taken early 1960, during the building of the Radical and Liberal Club. In 1998 the club was rebuilt as Pharoah's Night Club, shown opposite.

Co-op shops and the Ring O'Bells Inn in 1963.

Flour and flour stores in the days of home baking featured more prominently in everyday life and in shopping than they do today. Note (opposite) how the space to the left of this shop was later filled in.

'Island Corner'. The smaller shops were replaced by Francis Jordan House in 1989.

Silver Street in the 1960's.

MARKET STREET
EAST SIDE

NB. There are some differences between postal addresses and the numbers shown on the 2001 OS map. We show the postal address at the top of each column with the OS number, if different, in brackets.

2 (OS.6)
2001-1991 Digby Shoe Repairs
1991-1977 Marshall Shops
1976-1975 Empty
1974-1964 Coombes Footwear Repair
1961-1871 Johnsons Drug Store
1870-1868 Thomas Brocklebank

4 (OS.8)
2001-1986 Klik Film Processing
1985 Vacant
1982-1972 Sealand Foods

10
2001-1999 The Body Spa
1999-1993 The Kidz Shop
1990 Vacant
1990-1985 Justin Menswear
1985-1972 Geoffrey Davies
Outfitting

12
2001-1988 Supercigs
Tobacco/Confectionery
1986 Vacant
1986-1985 Checkers Menswear
1982-1975 Duncan Menswear
1974-19701 Chelsea Girl
1968-1964 Lewis Separates

─────────── Rebuilt 1963 ───────────

14
2001-1997 Now Fashions & Bridal
1997-1995 Now Ladies Fashion
1995-1993 Granada Televisions
1993-1970 Visionhire T.V. Rental
1969-1964 Rente Vision

4
1970-1962 Cambells Furniture
1961-1938 Grahams Furniture
1938-1936 Audley Charlesworth Furniture
1936-1868 H. Clegg and Son Ltd. Saddlers

6
1961-1868 Henry Clegg & Son
Leather Goods

8A
1961-1936 Crow Pork Butcher
1936-1906 A. Senior Son Tailors
1905 Miss Watson Haberdasher
1905 E. A. Ledger Printer
1899-1889 Henry Clegg
1885 Hy. B. Wilson
1884-1882 Edwin R. Fletcher
1871-1859 Geo. Hardcastle Boot M'

35
1863-1859 Isaac Clare
Clogger
1857-1855 Thomas Mellor
1854-1853 Stansby
1852-1851 John Weson
1849-1848 Wm. Mettrick
1847 James Heppenstall
Tailor
1846-1845 John Wilby

34
1863-1853 Geo. Fox Grocer
1852-1848 Sarah Dibb Hay Dealer
(Joseph)
1847-1845 James Sykes
Shopkeeper
1844-1841 Widow Collier
(Wm)

33
1863-1858 Hy. Milner Stationer
1857-1854 J. Asquith
1852-1842 Isaac Frudd
Hairdresser
1841-1839 Joseph Rollinson
1835 James Birkinshaw

COURT

32
1857-1841 Geo. Ambler Whitesmith

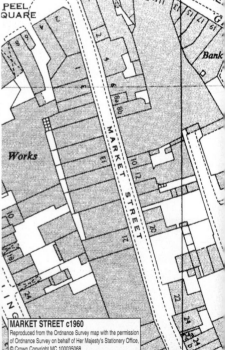

MARKET STREET c1960
Reproduced from the Ordnance Survey map with the permission of Ordnance Survey on behalf of Her Majesty's Stationery Office. © Crown Copyright MC 100035068

Charles Johnson moved to Number 2 Market Street from Queen Street in 1871 and the shop continued in the family for a ninety years.

16

2001-1999 Diary Dates
1999-1990 Intersports
1990-1986 Clarksons
    Fruit/Veg
1985-1982 Kew Cooked
    Meats
1981-1964 Stylo Footwear

8

1961-1930 Lilyan Ladies
    Outfitter
1929-1903 S. Eaton
    Hairdresser
1899 Thomas Mackeridge
1894-1891 John R. Thresh
1885 Isaac Clare Clogger

31

1867-1849 Charlesworth Co.
    Painters
1848 John Rushforth
1847-1841 Geo. Waterton

18-24

1982-1937 Marks &
    Spencers Ltd
1933 A. R. Copping
1932 B. Dwight Wallpaper
1929 A. Fell Furniture Bkr.
1912-1901 Samuel Cawthorn
    Furniture Bkr.
1900-1898 J. L. Gillis
1897-1884 Geo. Beaumont
    Paper Hanger
1883-1869 Isaac Clare
1868 Woodruff

30

1867-1851 Charles Binns
    Joiner
1850 Isaac Swift
1849-1839 Sarah Machin
1835 Richard Chappel

18-32 (OS.18-30)

2001-1982 Marks & Spencers
1978 Site for development of Marks & Spencers
1971 Vacant Site

10

1969-1947 S. Horner
    Footwear
1946-1930 Mrs. C. A. Lee
    Oufitter
1929-1916 John Wareham
    General Dealer

12

1969 N.C.B. Office
1968-1937 Hibbert Ashton
    & Youel Printers
1936-1922 Hlbbert, Murray Co.
    Printers
1922-1916 W. J. Deighton
    Printers

Above 14 and 16
1963-1961 R. J. Sabine
    J. Uprichard
1960-1952 J. Howcroft
1951-1942 Daybro Ltd.
1937-1920 J. G. &
    J. W. Deighton
    Dentists

14

1966-1961 G. Bell
    Tobacconist
1960-1940 Riley Co.
    Music Dealers
1939-1935 F. Diggle & Sc
    Furnishers
1934-1928 L. Francis
    Hairdresser
1927-1922 E. Edson
    Milliner
1922-1921 Mrs. C. Miller
    Milliner
1920-1916 R. Goulding
    Picture Frami

Rebuilt

10

1914-1884 Ann Hill

(Samuel)

1883-1879 Richard Smith
1878-1875 Wm. Briggs
1874 John Carrington
1872-1859 Mary Fletcher
1857-1854 Geo. Stringer
1852-1849 James Firth
    Clothes Broker
1845-1841 Ely Gill
1839- Brown
1835-1833 Hy. Jenkinson

12

1914-1913 J. Mulvey
1912 M. Lodge Picture Framer
1910-1889 Thomas Ibberson
    Picture Framer
1888-1887 Thomas G. Harper
1886-1885 Francis Hutchinson
1884-1883 Servants Home
1882 Charles Curtis
1874-1861 John Bygate
    Boot-Shoe Maker

28

1860 John Charlesworth
1859 Martha Bradley
1857-1849 Ann Price
1847-1846 John Coates
1845- Josiah Large
1844-1841 Wm. Thompson
    Book Keeper
1838-1835 John Matthewman
1833 Mrs Hammerton

14

1914-1885 J. Wareham
    General Dealer
1883-1881 John Taylor
1880-1873 Ellen Spear

(Geo)

1872 Wm. Ashworth Tailor
1870 Geo. Fairclough
1869 John Hy. Atkinson

27

1868 James C. Shaw
1867-1864 Hy. Milner
1863-1860 Joseph Fish
    Picture Framer
1859-1845 George Ambler
    Whitesmith
1844 Charles Tonge
1843-1842 John Bennett
1841 John Ostcliffe
Registrar of Births & Deaths
1839 John Holdham
1835-1833 Geo. Shepherd

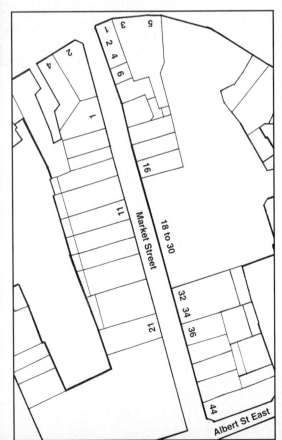

Market Street 2001.

Craftsmen stand in front of the premises where their leather goods were made and sold. The advent of the car meant the disappearance of the horse and the subsequent reduced importance of the saddler. The properties still survive in 2001.

Number 4 to 8A before the alterations of 1960. Now numbers 6 to 14.

2001-1982 Marks & Spencer

1971- Vacant Site
16
1969-1961 Stone Dri Weather Wear
1960-1936 Margaret Gowns
1935 J. W. Deighton
1934 Mrs. S. Ware
1933 L.E. Rothwell
1932-1928 M. Copley
1927-1910 Mrs. Burns
        Electrical Engineer
1909 Joseph Wainwright
1908-1906 Thomas E. B. Green
1905 R. Gages Confectioner
1902-1901 Miss C. Ibberson
        Confectioner
1900-1893 Hy. Hinchcliffe
1892-1878 Josiah Franshaw

(Samuel)

1877-1869 Richard Smith

26
1868-1863 Charles Ledger
1863-1862 B.B.C.S.
1862 Edward Jaques
1861 M. Thompson
1860 Thomas Beever
1859-1837 John Charlesworth
        Linen Manufacturer
1835 Barley and Thompson

34/36 (OS.32/34)
2001-1989 Adams Childrens Wear
1988-1980 Wigfalls T.V. Electrical, Audio
1980-1963 Spiers Fashion Accessories
Rebuild 1962

18
1955-1890 J. Kirwan
1889-1884 Sarah Rooke
1883-1868 Frances Hutchinson

25
1867-1858 Abraham Ashworth
        Tailor
1857-1844 Geo. Naylor
1842-1841 Eliz. Smith
        Shopkeeper
1839 Roberts
1835 Charles Bailey

20
1961-1936 F. M. Rickson Herbalist
1935-1892 Miss L. Dixon Herbalist
1891-1853 John S. Ingall Herbalist

24
1852-1841 Thomas Smith
        Rate Collector
1839 Wm. Thompson

38 (OS.36)
2001-1986 Lunn Poly Ltd.
        Travel Agent
1986 March Menswear
1985-1972 Telefusion

40 (OS.38)
2001-1998 The P.D.S.A. shop
1997-1996 Vacant
1996-1990 Colourvision T.V.
1988 Quote Hairdressers
1985-1972 March The Tailor

1967-1966 B.B.C.S. Sleepware Dept.
Rebuilt 1966

Yard

The last occupiers of number 14 and 16 before demolition.

Numbers 10 to 16 in 1960. These properties were demolished around 1970 and redeveloped as the extended Marks & Spencer, seen opposite in 2001.

Numbers 18 and 20 before being rebuilt in 1962. Mr Kirwan, hairdresser, occupied number 18 for sixty-five years and number 20 was a herbalists for nearly twice this time.

The east side of Market Street after rebuilding in 1962 and 1966.

Numbers 24 and 24A before the 1972 rebuilding.

42 (OS.40)	44 (OS.42)	46 (OS.44)	Albert St. East	48 (OS.46/48)	50
2001-1993 Best Jean Co.	2001-1998 N.C.H. Charity Shop	2001-1994 Barnsley Skil Shop		2001-1992 Kennedy Travel	2001-1998 P.J.'s Coffee Bar Restaurant
1991 Cardshops Cards	1997 Vacant	1994-1986 Milletts Camping		1992-1991 Sue Ryder Charity Shop	1998-1996 Childstyle
1990 Vacant	1996 Maze Music	1985-1972 Army Stores		1991-1986 Rumbelows Audio/T.V. Electrical	1996-1992 Sue Ryder Charity Shop
1990-1972 Card Shop	1995-1989 Computer Store			1985-1973 Bambers Ladies/Childrens Wear	1992-1971 Kennedy Travel
	1988-1986 The Gold House Jeweller			1973-1972 Vernon Fashions	
	1985 Vacant				
	1982-1976 Peter Ashley Leatherwear				
	1976-1972 Wine Ways				

22	24	24A		26
1969-1962 BBCS Optical Dept.	1960-1953 BBCS Handbags	1960 B.B.C.S. Cock Chicken	1969-1960 B.B.C.S. Nurseries	1969-1950 B.B.C.S. Nurseries
1960-1923 Union of Distributive & Allied Workers	1952-1941 L.A. Joy Draper	1940 Mrs. C. A. Lee	1955-1941 A. Hepworth	1944-1935 A. Cawthorne
1923-1922 A. Hepworth	1940-1937 Mrs. C. A. Lee	1937-1921 Barnsley Association for the Blind	1940 Mrs. C. A. Lee	1935-1915 Thomas Brown Pikelet Maker
1921 Mrs. Taylor	1933 Barnsley Corporation Welfare Centre		1937-1926 Barnsley Association for the Blind	1914-1907 Wm. Charlesworth
1916-1884 John Taylor	1915-1884 Geo. Charlton		1920-1919 Iveson and Son	
1883- Wm. Hy. Horne	1883 Bell and Bray		1918 J. Kaye	
1880 Hannah Stringer	1882-1869 Edward Hammond Temperance Hotel		1917 Mrs. Haigh	
1879-1877 John Wm. Dobson	**Crown Inn**		1916 C. Dyke	
1875 Emily Huntington	1869-1863 Edward Hammond			
1874-1857 Saml. H. Neatby	1862-1861 Samuel Dyson			
	1861-1860 Thomas Coward			
23	1859 S. Mason			
(Joseph)	1857 R. R. Alderson			
1854-1850 Thomas Wainwright Surgeon	1856-1854 Thomas G. Hamer			
1847-1835 Thomas Dale Auctioneer	1851 Wm. Horne Stay Manufacturer			
1833 M. Carter	1850-1830 Wm. Ridsdale Carrier			

Yard

Workshop in Taylor's Yard.

Number 22, for most of its life a private house, was pulled down in 1970, when these properties were replaced by those shown above.

52

2001-1991 K.M. Travel

(1991-1983 K.M. Travel leased half the shop, numbered 52A)

1991-1990 Moneysave Household Goods

1990-1986 Vacant

1985-1982 Supasnaps

1982 Tandem Footwear

1980-1962 Leighs Footwear

54

2001-1975 Barnardos Charity Shop

1975-1962 Hagenbachs Confectioners

56

2001-1999 Market Street Butchers (Andrew Cleland)

1999-1996 Andrew Cleland Butcher

1996-1973 Worsleys Butchers

1973-1966 Stuart Jubb Butcher

58

2001-2000 Car Phone Warehouse Mobile Phone Shop

2000-1974 Tandy Electrical

1973- Mr Frost Hairdresser

60

2001 Eyecare Barnsley

2001-1973 Cooperative Society Opticians

28A

1961-1930 E. Sugden Furniture

1929-1930 A. Smith

28

1961-1910 J. Hinchliffe Health Stores

(C.E.)

1909-1907 A. Watson

1906 J Heald

1905 Geo. Derrick

1904-1902 W. Buttery

1900-1893 Arthur Raynor

1892-1888 John Green

1887-1868 Emma Greenwood

30

1966-1958 Crow Pork Butcher

1957-1935 Art Crafts

1933 F. Turner Watchmaker

1931-1915 J. H. Simpson Watchmaker

1914-1912 F. Potter Draper

1910-1911 Barnsley Rubber Co.

1909 L. Nelson

1906-1889 Charles Wilkinson

1887-1875 Joseph Moss

1874-1871 John Mason

32

1970-1911 R. Jackson Petshop

1910-1860 House

34

1959-1850 House

Mr Jackson's Pet Shop lasted for sixty years, until all these properties were redeveloped in the early 1970s.

BBCS shops at the top of Market Street in the 1960s.

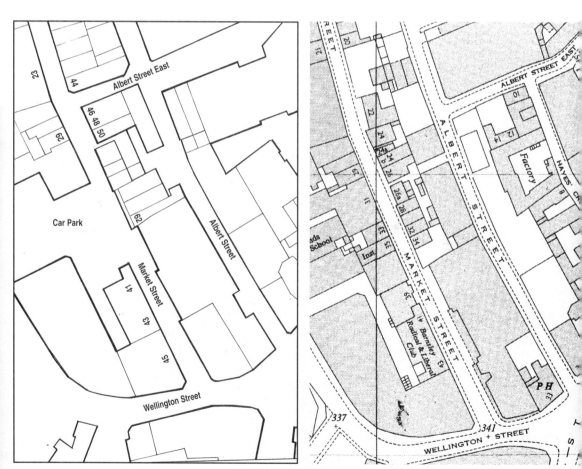

MARKET STREET in 2001 (left) and c1960 (right).
Reproduced from the Ordnance Survey map with the permission of Ordnance Survey on behalf of Her Majesty's Stationery Office, © Crown Copyright MC 100035068

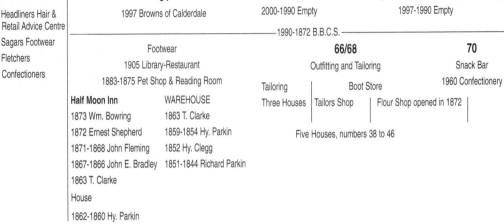

62	64	2001-2000 Aphrodite's Health & Beauty	2001-1997 Barnsley Shopmobility
2001-1994 Headliners Hair & Retail Advice Centre	1997 Browns of Calderdale	2000-1990 Empty	1997-1990 Empty

1990-1872 B.B.C.S.

62	64	66/68	70
1994-1987 Sagars Footwear	Footwear	Outfitting and Tailoring	Snack Bar
1986-1972 Fletchers	1905 Library-Restaurant		1960 Confectionery
Confectioners	1883-1875 Pet Shop & Reading Room		

			66/68		70
	Half Moon Inn	WAREHOUSE	Tailoring	Boot Store	
	1873 Wm. Bowring	1863 T. Clarke	Three Houses	Tailors Shop	Flour Shop opened in 1872
	1872 Ernest Shepherd	1859-1854 Hy. Parkin			
	1871-1868 John Fleming	1852 Hy. Clegg	Five Houses, numbers 38 to 46		
	1867-1866 John E. Bradley	1851-1844 Richard Parkin			
	1863 T. Clarke				
	House				
	1862-1860 Hy. Parkin				

It was from this property that the shop of the Barnsley British Cooperative Society evolved.

Lower part of the Grocery Department in 1961.

72

Restaurant Grocers

Provision Store

Warehouse

1874-1864 Barnsley British
          Cooperative Society

1861-1859 James Rogers

1858-1833 Henry Parkin

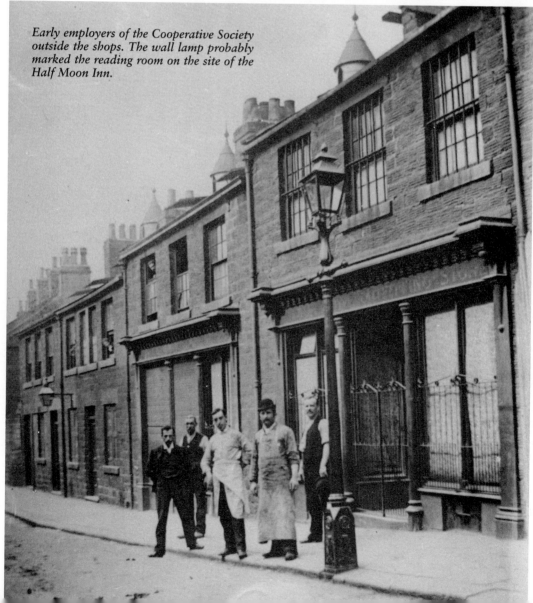

Early employers of the Cooperative Society outside the shops. The wall lamp probably marked the reading room on the site of the Half Moon Inn.

The Society's first confectioners and dining rooms which were between the grocery department at the corner of Market Street and New Street, and the Trafalgar Hotel in New Street.

The shops standing on the first site purchased in the 1890s by the Barnsley British
Cooperative Society. Seen in the 1960s with the more modern shops beyond.

19

2001-1993 Discount Shoe Zone

1993-1991 Benson Shoes

1991-1972 Roseby's

1970 Granada

1962-1960 A. Isherwood Ltd.
Television

17

-April 2001 The Barnsley Dental
Health Centre

2001-1999 Whitecross Dental Care

1999-1991 Windsmoor Ladies
Fashions

1991-1990 Vacant

1990-1988 Next to Nothing Ladies
Fashions

1986 Vacant

1985-1982 Lady at Lord John
Ladies Fashions

1980-1960 Bradmore Fashions

15

2001-1991 Oxfam Charity Shop

1991-1978 Curtess Footwear

1978-1960 Freeman Hardy & Willis

13

Closed 2001

2001-2000 King Pie
Takeaway

2000-1996 Best Sellers

1995 Vacant

1991-1960 Home Farm
Products

11

2001-1998 The Cancer
Research Campaign

1998-1976 Leopold Bullion

1976-1960 Bellmans Wool

Rebuilt

1912-1886 Alfred Hudson

Carriage Builder

1863 Wm. Neatly Saw Mill

1861-1847 Joseph Shaw

Hope Saw Mill

1846 Thomas Dale

1845-1844 Clarkson & Dale

1842-1830 Deacon & Co.

Numbers 3-9. The first occupiers of the shops which were opened in 1960. Above, shops numbering from 13 downwards in 2001.

9	7	5	3	1
2001-2000d Card Warehouse	2001-1999 Greggs of Yorkshire Bakers	2001-1998 The Phone People P.L.C.	2001-1996 Charlie's Hair Salon	2001-1999 Card Factory
2000-1990 Andy's Records	1999-1976 Thurlstons Bakers	1998-1995 Clinton Cards	1995 Quit Charity Shop	1999-1993 Reel Star Amusements
1990 Vacant	1976-1962 Halfords Confectioners	1995 Carlton Cards	1995-1980 Segal's Curtains	1993-1986 Jeanery Leatherwear
1988-1973 Peter Lord Footwear	1961-1960 Frances Fair	1991-1963 Memory Lane Cards	1980-1978 Vacant	1985 Crash Fashion
1973-1960 Noel's Fashions		1962-1960 Salisbury Handbags	1978-1968 Crockatt's Cleaners	1982 Jeanmania Leatherwear
			1967-1960 Martins Cleaners	1980-1974 Mason's Footwear
Rebuilt				1973-1969 Henry Fenton Outfitters
				1968 Smart Weston Outfitters
				1964-1960 John Manners Ltd Outfitters

1960-1857 M. Lowrance Son Ltd. Ironmongers

Rear of Crown Hotel
See Peel Square

Left, a general view from Peel Square. in 2001.

The original shop of M. Lowrance and Son Ltd., was at the corner of Peel Square and Market Street. When the corner was developed the firm moved to a new shop which stood on the site of number one Market Street, seen in the late 1950s.

Looking down towards Peel Square in the late 1950s. All these properties were demolished and rebuilt in 1960. The tiled frontage to the left is number 23.

Numbers 11 to 15. *On the site during the last quarter of the nineteenth century were two cottages and a blacksmiths forge run by John Colbeck.*

Numbers 17 to 21. *These shops stand on the site of a carriage works which followed a saw mill. The saw mill stretched between Market Street and Wellington Street.*

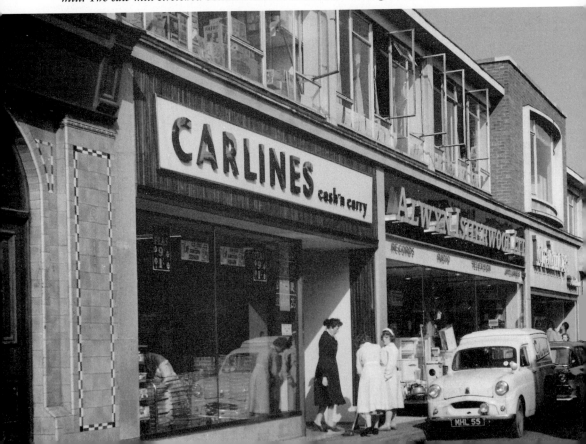

29

2001-1974 Dolland & Aitcheson
Optician

1974-1971 Farmhouse Spit Roast

1971-1951 Bernards Fabric

1950-1947 Burneys Fabrics

1944-1929 Epworth and Hall

1938 E. Rogers

1937-1933 P. Spensley Florist

1933-1923 A. P. Bacon

1922-1918 A. Carlton Hairdresser

1913-1912 Wm. Charlesworth

1911 Hy. W. Carlisle

1910 C. Briggs

1909-1895 Joseph Askham

1894-1862 Robt. Greenwood
Plumber

1860 Geo. Gelder

1859 Geo. Stringer

1857-1835 Mary Ridsdale

(William)

2001-1985 Shoefayre Footware

1985 rebuilt

27

1982-1968 Boardmans Furniture

1967-1963 H. Crossland
Music Store

1962-1956 Marcova Ladies
Fashions

1955-1929 Ward and Hoey
Milliners

25

1982-1963 Boardmans Furniture

1962-1935 Crowther Sugden
Furniture

1935-1928 E. Sanderson

1928-1922 C. Miller

23

2001-1991 What Everyone Wants

Rebuilt 1990

1990-1920 B.B.C.S. Hosiery
Ladies/Gents Wear

1920-1888 J. E. Vero
Printing Works

21

-2001 The Works

2001-1996 First Stop Stationery

1996-1990 Worralls
Stationery/Toys

1989 The Wool Shop

1988 Vacant

1986-1971 Minerva Cafe

1971-1970 Fine Fair

1969-1960 Carlines Self Service

Number 23 was sometimes still referred to as Vero's Printing Works. It was built in 1888 by J. E. Vero who had a shop in Queen Street near the Three Cranes Hotel. Above, as rebuilt in 1990. To its left numbers 25 and 27 rebuilt as Shoefayre in 1985.

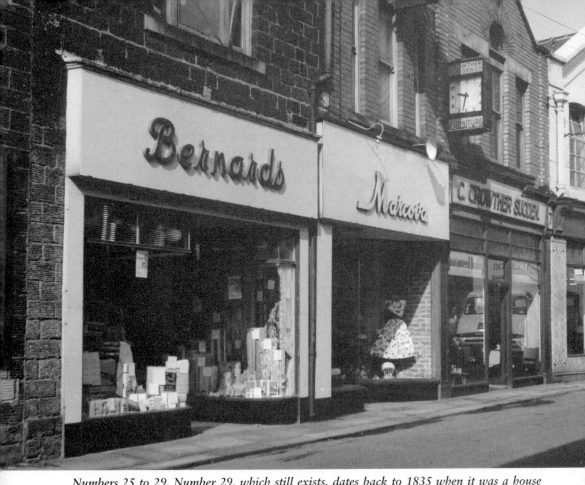

Numbers 25 to 29. Number 29, which still exists, dates back to 1835 when it was a house occupied by Wm. Ridsdale. The other two were added as shop property in 1920, and were rebuilt in 1985.

Number 31 in 2001.

2001-1973 Car Park

1920 Houses Number 13 and 15 | 1960 Numbers 9 and 11 Friends Adult School Social Centre

31

2001-2000 Your More Store
200-1995 Catalogue Shop
1995 Vacant
1990-1978 B.B.C.S. T.V./Electrical
1973-1915 B.B.C.S. Kitchen Ware

1912-1874 W. E. Brady Bakehouse
1873-1862 School (J.H. Lupton)
(John M. Mossley)
1860-1836 New Methodist Connexion School

1912-1874 W. E. Brady Shop
1873-1852 Franklin Institute

The car park which has replaced 33 to 39.

The Co-op kitchenware shop, number 31, was built in 1915, replacing old school property of the New Methodist Connexion part of which had become a bakehouse and part of which was used as a meeting place by the Franklin Society. The buildings beyond, 33-39, now demolished as seen in on the previous page and the inset photograph opposite.

134,700 MEMBERS ENJOY CO-OP

2001-1998 Wellington House Barnsley Council Building			
1998-1995 Vacant			
45	**43**	**41**	**39**
1991-1990 Kitchen Warehouse	1991- Larif Leather Fashions	1990 Co-op Travel Agents	2001-1973 Car Park
	1991-1990 Bookshop	1986-1973 B.B.C.S. Chemists	1962-1946 Art Crafts Ltd.
	1990 Vacant	1972-1963 B.B.C.S. Wallpaper	1941-1894 R. Snowden Plumber
	1986-1973 Barnsley British Coop Soc. Jewellery - Butchers	1960-1892 Radical & Liberal Club	1893 J. H. Squire Corn & Potato Merchant
		1909 Reopened after fire	1889 Brook Noblett
	1868-1860 Wm. Dennis | 1868-1860 Ed. Hall	1887-1870 George Hardcastle House - Shop - Rag Warehouse	1887-1867 Geo. Hardcastle
			1866-1856 Henry Clegg

The staff pose outside the premises of R. Snowden and Son

The guard rail was an attractive piece of iron work.

Numbers 41 onwards in 2001.

LIMITED

ESTABLISHED &

FOR GOOD SERVICE AND EXCELLENT FARE
VISIT
THE ARCADIAN
RESTAURANT.
OPPOSITE →

The corner is dominated by the Co-operative Buildings, now Barnsley Council offices.